A Collectors Guide To

David Winter Cottages

Edited by John Hughes

John Hughes

Published in the United Kingdom
by
Collectables Publishing Limited

ACKNOWLEDGMENTS

Special thanks to David Winter for reading parts of and commenting on the manuscript, Glenn Blackman for design and photography, Dan Byrne for allowing me to reproduce photographs belonging to John Hine Limited, and John Hine for giving me the oppotunity to acquire the knowledge. Many others helped to compile this book by supplying information over a period of time, especially for the secondary market price guide — my thanks to them all. Additional thanks to: Ken Armke, Ted Camhi, Mary Carr, Sherrie Carr, Jim & Bonnie Coates, David Cohen, Pia Colon, Simon Connolly, Rita Costello, Tracey Ford, Brian Gourlay, Ann Hamlet, Pat Hinckle, Stuart & Sally (they know who they are), James Howton, Heather Lavender, Matthew Luzny, Nick Emerson, Bill Mesa, Bev Munro, Betty Page, Brian Pannaman, Kevin Pearson, Annette Power, Tanya Price, Tanzel Rousey, Jim Summers, Glen Womack, Bill Younger — and not forgetting Danny Boy.

Front cover picture: The resin painting master of Plum Cottage, originated by Kerry Agar in September 1993.

Produced by Creativehouse, Aldershot

Introduction

Collectable miniature cottages did not exist before 1980. It was then that two people with complementary skills, John Hine and David Winter, hit on the right idea at the right time and created a new market with their David Winter Cottages. Looking back it seems surprising that miniature cottages had not been successfully marketed before. The fact is that people had tried, but only in ceramic which cannot hold very fine detail, *the* most appealing characteristic of the genre. Adopting the technique of crystacal cast in silicon moulds allowed this detail to be retained and recreated with relative speed and simplicity. Most importantly, the technique has enabled David's original sculptures to be recreated at an affordable price.

The popularity of David Winter Cottages is a credit to David's sculpting and John's entrepreneurial skills. Yet ironically it is the tiny failures along the way, especially during the first few years, that have ensured meteoric success in the secondary market, where retired (discontinued) pieces are resold for much more than the original issue price. Sabrina's Cottage and the Double Oast, poor sellers made in small quantities and dropped because nobody wanted to buy them, are now worth a great deal of money and are highly sought after by collectors. The failures have helped to generate the notion that David Winter Cottages are a bona fide investment.

Latterly, awareness of this trait has led to limited edition pieces and a policy of regular retirements; sowing seeds for the secondary market of tomorrow. Hence the need for a price guide. "How are my investments doing?" is a question that most collectors wish to have answered. The reply is that like the stock market, the secondary market in collectables fluctuates; and when prices are low the shrewd are buying, not selling.

Newly retired pieces are constantly revitalising the market, as is the move towards limited edition pieces such as Mad Baron Fourthrite's Folly (1992) and Horatio Pernickety's Amorous Intent (1993). Collectors and dealers are also becoming more aware of the difference in price between early and late versions of the same piece. Tudor Manor House (1981) is a fine example; barely a handful of 'Mould 1' pieces exist and are very rare, whilst later 'Mould 3' pieces are to be found in most collections, having remained in production unaltered for seven years. The value differentials between 'Moulds' is only just beginning to emerge with any clarity, due primarily to lack of information.

The acquisition of John Hine Limited by Media Arts Group Inc. in December 1993 will no doubt have a significant affect on the future of David Winter Cottages. Logic dictates that an American organisation will lead what was previously an entirely British company in a new direction: more restricted edition sizes, perhaps; consistent marketing strategy; a change in retirement policy — all things that will create the valuable retired David Winter Cottages of the future, including pieces David hasn't yet sculpted. Exciting things are clearly in store just around the corner.

However, this book is a summary of what has gone before, not a prediction of what is to come, and the intention is to inform collectors by reporting facts. It covers David Winter's output from the very beginning up until Spring 1994, including all current, retired, Guild and special pieces, in as much detail as possible. In many ways it is an update of my The David Winter Cottages Handbook 1992/93, though much effort has been made to adopt a fresh approach to the subject — and indeed much has happened during the past two years.

John Hughes
April 1994

About the Author

Born in 1956, John Hughes was brought up in Sutton Coldfield, a town in the English Midlands. He studied music at Royal Holloway College, Surrey, and gained an Honours Degree in 1977. For six years he worked at Harrods department store, London, selling pianos and synthesizers, primarily as a Yamaha consultant. In 1985 he published a self-tuition book on how to play electronic keyboards which is still in print.

In 1984 he met John Hine and collaborated with him on a variety of musical projects on a freelance basis. The following year he joined John Hine Limited to assist in developing a music recording side of the company, but soon found himself becoming involved in the world of David Winter Cottages. He was involved in the Collectors Guild from its inception in 1987, primarily as Assistant Editor of the Guild magazine, *Cottage Country* , and worked on every issue until leaving the company in December 1993. For two years he was

also Manager of the Guild in the United Kingdom. During this time he acquired an in-depth knowledge of David Winter Cottages.

He wrote *The David Winter Cottages Handbook* in 1992, the first official price guide ever published, and a year later produced *Inside David Winter Cottages* , a compilation of background information and stories about the Cottages, including a long interview with David Winter himself. Since leaving John Hine Limited he has established his own company, Collectables Publishing Limited, to produce a series of price guides for collectables, and this book is its first publication.

John still retains an active interest in music whenever possible and for ten years played piano and vibraphones in a dance band with members of the Royal Philharmonic Orchestra. He and his wife, Chris, live in Surrey with their two daughters, Helen and Alice.

Contents

Section One

The David Winter Story

The story begins in the summer of 1979 when John Hine sold the garden centre he had been running for a number of years and began to look around for something new to occupy his highly creative mind. Heraldry had always fascinated him and he decided to develop an idea which had occurred to him long before — to produce a series of sculptures of heraldic shields.

With this in mind he approached Faith Winter, whose garden sculptures John had stocked at the garden centre. Faith is a busy sculptor, highly regarded by her peers and much sought-after for prestigious commissions. She did not have time to consider the heraldry project but mentioned it to her younger son, David, and suggested he should consider the idea.

David Winter was twenty at the time (born 18 December 1958), a shy young man who, like his sister Alice, had inherited his mother's artistic gift. From a very early age he had been watching Faith at work in her studio, absorbing her skills and developing an eye for three-dimensional forms. In 1979 he was making a tentative living selling ceramic tiles from a stall in Guildford market. (He decorated the tiles by placing them on a potter's wheel and spinning them round to produce a variety of spiral designs.) The heraldry idea came as a welcome challenge and

David set to work on a test piece. At that time he lived at home with his parents and used an old coalshed in the garden as a studio. There he sculpted the test piece, using modelling wax, from which he then made a mould of silicon rubber. From the mould he made a cast using *Crystacal* , this being the trade name of a grade of gypsum plaster produced by the British Gypsum company. The wax, silicon rubber and plaster were all materials familiar to him; Faith Winter uses *Crystacal* for her own work.

When the time came to show John the piece David was very nervous, not from any doubts about his own skills but because he wasn't sure if he had created what John had in mind. But his anxiety was unfounded; John was delighted with the piece and realised he had found the right person for the project.

They set to work in earnest, using a disused coalshed in David's parents' garden as their studio and office. Between them they could research, sculpt and cast the plaques — but someone was still needed to paint the white casts. So John placed an advertisement in his local newspaper and was lucky enough to receive a reply from Audrey White, a painter specialising in miniatures who had raised a family and was now available for work again. Having asked her to paint a test piece, John knew he need look no further.

It was now September and David, John and Audrey worked on the heraldic plaques through October and November and into December. Then in the week prior to Christmas, the busiest shopping time of the year, the plaques went on exhibit for the very first time, in a hall in the centre of Guildford. Their expectations were high; but sadly sales were not. Number of plaques sold — zero.

Heraldic plaques were clearly not going to set the public alight with enthusiasm and

Photos courtesy of John Hine Ltd.

Left: Faith Winter's Prince Charles Bust
Right: One of the unsuccessful heraldic plaques. Note the owl.

in the first month of 1980 they had been replaced by a new project. Faith Winter had sculpted a bust of Prince Charles, who in early 1980 was an eligible bachelor surrounded by intense speculation regarding his marital plans. David was making casts of the bust in the coalshed and John was offering them for sale in three different finishes. The response from shops was less than enthusiastic; it was an excellent likeness (Faith Winter is renowned for her uncanny ability in that respect) but the bust was not something that gift stores thought would sell well. Furthermore it was slightly top heavy and tended to topple over.

One day John was in St Catherine's dock, near Tower Bridge in London, trying to interest a gift shop owner in the bust. Having failed in his objective he asked the gentleman to explain to him what *would* sell if busts of Prince Charles wouldn't. "Cottages," came the reply and the man pointed out a ceramic butter dish designed in the style of a thatched cottage which was particularly popular with his customers. John took one away with him and before the day was out it was in David's hands.

From the very beginning David and John both found the idea extremely appealing. The cottage homes and workplaces of England are a romantic subject and the nostalgia they generate for bygone days, a charming world of rustic bliss, is an emotion shared by many. Most of all, the idea offered a wealth of sculptural possibilities.

A mill was decided upon as a test piece — a building very much part of a past era; romantic and old-fashioned. David worked slowly, sculpting with matchboxes hidden beneath the modelling wax because he didn't have enough to fill it out. He used matchsticks to represent beams on the walls and strips of lace to create a patterned effect on the crown of the thatch. The piece turned out to be more than just a cottage; the base extended to include a front garden with a fence, an expanse of river, bushes and an outhouse reached by a bridge. On the front edge he added a rectangular plaque which read: THE MILL HOUSE, ENGLAND, © DAVID WINTER.

When the sculpture was finished, David made a mould of it and cast two pieces which he painted himself. They decided to try their luck with a local shop and on the morning of 10th March John took the pieces to Guildford and offered them to a giftware shop at 201 High Street called *David Windsor* on a 'sale-or-return' basis. The shop owner was not optimistic about making a quick sale but nevertheless placed the cottages on display, pricing them at £7.50 each. Happily he was proved wrong; one of the pieces sold that very afternoon.

When John and David received a phone call telling them the news and asking for some more cottages, they were ecstatic. After two false starts their business venture had eventually left the starting blocks. Celebrations were in order, the cost of which amounted to double the figure they had earned from their first sale!

With spirits lifted, things now moved with a sudden burst of speed. *Spectrum Gallery* in Dorking (10 miles east of Guildford) became the second stockist, followed shortly by *Bell, Book & Candle* near Hampton Court, and within a week John had interested half-a-dozen shops in stocking The Mill House. Meanwhile David not only cast the pieces but also sculpted three more in rapid succession — Dove Cottage, Three Ducks Inn and The Forge, in that order. As with The Mill House, David incorporated external objects into the wax such as buckets and an anvil from a pack of modelling accessories — objects he would later sculpt himself as his technique developed. By the end of April he had remodelled the original Mill House by cutting away the scenic base, created Little Mill and Little Forge from their larger 'parents', and sculpted a set of 'Mini Cottages' which soon became known as the Tiny Series.

Audrey was now involved in painting all the pieces, initially batches of three or four at a time, though the numbers gradually increased with demand. When David had cast a batch, John took them home with him and left them on his storage heater overnight to dry out. Very early in the morning he would leave them in the cat box in Audrey's back garden for her to paint during the day. When they were finished she placed them back in the cat box last thing at night and John would collect them early the next morning, replacing them with another batch of unpainted pieces. It was a convenient routine which allowed John the maximum amount of time at the coalshed and visiting shops and gave Audrey the whole day to paint.

As the year progressed the workload became too great for just three people. John hired Anthony Wyatt to help him sell to shops and Audrey trained two new painters. Early the following year David Gravelle also joined the team. By the end of 1980 David had also sculpted Market Street, Little Market, The Winemerchant, Quayside, The Coaching Inn and Rose Cottage. Just before Christmas David celebrated his twenty-first birthday.

1981 began very differently from 1980 with the search for new premises to house a budding cottage industry. Even with an extension the coalshed had served its purpose and David had resorted in the cold midst of winter to sculpting on his parents' dining room table (Tudor Manor House). John found an empty shop at 19 Ash Street to serve as studio, office and production workshop. David worked well here and, starting with Single, Double and Triple Oast, proceeded to develop the true characteristics of David Winter Cottages — rickety roofs, irregular walls, outsized chimneys, precise and intricate detail. He achieved his objective in Stratford House, the first piece, in David's opinion, to demonstrate his mature style. Before 1981 was out he had excelled himself by producing a masterpiece — The Village.

Demand for David Winter Cottages was increasing rapidly. The *Chinacraft* chain of stores provided John Hine with his first substantial order and others followed. The network of stockists was spreading further and further afield, amongst them the prestigious London store, Harrods. More mouldmakers,

casters and painter were taken on and in 1982 another new building was acquired at Hendon Road, Bordon. David moved his studio there and remained for about a year until he started working from his newly acquired home, situated next door to his parents' house and just yards from the coalshed.

With technique and style firmly established, he was now creating a wide range of pieces, including some of his most enduringly popular pieces — House On Top (1982), Fairytale Castle (1982), The Bakehouse (1983) and The Bothy (1983).

Although David Winter Cottages did not become widely available in North America until a permanent office had been established in 1983 in Vancouver, Canada, under the control of Joe McCaig, tentative steps had been made in that direction the year before and a small number of pieces found their way into US stores. *The English Center* in Bellvue, Washington, was one of them; during a trip to England, the owner, Christine Kuyper, saw David Winter Cottages in a gift shop and tracked John Hine down to place an order. The Cottages were also on sale in several stores in Connecticut at about the same time.

Between 1983 and 1988 David Winter Cottages became a household name. David continued to sculpt one fine piece after another — The Parsonage (1984), Falstaff's Manor (1985), There Was a Crooked House (1986) — all of which could be purchased in stores on both sides of the Atlantic, and more and more so worldwide. Furthermore, David Winter Cottages had created their own band of enthusiastic collectors who were keen to acquire each new piece as it became available. David Winter Cottages had become 'collectable.'

David himself had long since ceased to

be his own mouldmaker and caster; these were now whole departments. His time was free to sculpt and sculpt alone. In 1984 he converted an outhouse in his garden into a studio, and there he has worked ever since; although nowadays he also works on a table inside his cottage (especially when there is a cricket match on TV!).

John on the other hand was now in charge of a substantial company with all the concomitant responsibilities which this entails. His working day had become a case of juggling entrepreneurial and creative matters with financial and administrative duties. Fortunately he has always been an early riser, habitually behind his desk before most people are awake.

In early 1985 John acquired the first of a series of premises in Woolmer Way, Bordon, less than a mile from Hendon Road, which allowed him the space to make more cottages for the ever increasing demand, notably in the United States. The following year, he purchased a group of dilapidated old buildings on Eggars Hill, Aldershot, and proceeded to convert them into offices and a visitor's centre. He also moved into the house next door and gradually combined his home into part of the complex. The main attraction had been a seventeenth century barn which was restored inside a brick and glass shell.

In response to the rising number of letters and phonecalls from collectors wanting more information about the Cottages and the man who sculpts them, John established the David Winter Cottages Collectors Guild in 1987. Not only does it provide information but also special pieces sculpted by David exclusively for Guild members.

In the same year David sculpted Ebenezer Scrooge's Counting House, a piece available only for the Christmas period. Its popularity was phenomenal and John could still have been fulfilling orders a year later. It was the first of a series of Christmas 'specials' available for a limited period only, all of which have been equally successful. 'Limited availability' brought a whole new aspect to collecting David Winter Cottages in the late 1980s with the demand for discontinued pieces generating an active secondary market. Since then the retirement of pieces and the production of limited edition pieces has developed greater significance.

By 1989 Woolmer Way had grown as

much as it could and new workshops were established in Southampton, Newcastle-upon-Tyne and, most significantly, Wrexham in North Wales. It was in effect the beginning of a relocation programme and by the end of 1993 the Bordon workshops had closed down altogether; all David Winter Cottages are now made in Wrexham, with Southampton providing painting facilities only. Similarly in North America in 1988, John Hine Studios moved from Vancouver into the United States, establishing the offices in Houston, Texas, which have remained their headquarters until 1994.

These concerns have always been John's territory. David has kept a low profile and concentrated on sculpting, making occasional appearances at stores and shows to sign pieces and meet collectors. The 1990s have not seen any waning in his ability to create fresh and imaginative cottages. CASTLE IN THE AIR (1991) was a masterly work, and Horatio Pernickety's Amorous Intent (1993) another highly inventive piece. In delightful contrast The English Village (1993/94) seems like a nostalgic harking back to the style of the early 1980s, as if a reminder of the themes which first permeated the first David Winter Cottages.

1993 saw two pieces sculpted for exclusive availability at special events — Arches Thrice for a tour of North America which David made in March and April, and The Castle Cottage of Warwick for a two day Carnival held in October.

Then in December 1993 came the most substantial change in the history of David Winter Cottages — the acquisition of John Hine Limited by Media Arts Group Inc., an American company which has rapidly become a considerable force in the field of collectables during the 1990s. In early 1994 it is too soon to appreciate the extent of how this will affect David Winter Cottages. But changes there will be, as news that John Hine Studios in Houston will be relocated to San Jose in California, indicates.

Fourteen years after David sculpted Mill House in the cramp confines of a coalshed, a new and exciting future has clearly dawned for David Winter Cottages.

Collecting Cottages

"The more you know about something the more you appreciate it." Is that a quote from somewhere, or did I just make it up? Either way, it's a true statement and the following information will hopefully be of benefit in learning about both the pieces *and* the market they have created.

John Hine Studios - The Manufacturer

'David Winter Cottages' is the trading name for a range of miniature cottages produced by *John Hine Limited*. They have always been made in Great Britain — for most of the 1980s exclusively in England until the Wrexham workshop opened in North Wales which has become the prime location in the 1990s. In the mid-1980s the company name was extended to *The Studios and Workshops of John Hine Limited* and this title is currently used on the backstamps of all pieces. The name reflects the two diverse aspects of the company's activity — the highly creative and artistic side (studio) and the manufacturing element (workshops). The change also coincided with the development of further ranges of miniature sculptures by a pool of artists whom John Hine has nurtured to complement the 'flagship' range of David Winter Cottages — including Malcolm Cooper, Jenny Baker, Hilary Macdonald, Janet King, Paul Williams, Patrick Gates and Christopher Lawrence. Primarily due to the influence of the USA, the name is commonly abbreviated to *John Hine Studios* and this is used mainly throughout this book for simplicity.

How Cottages Are Made

DAVID'S ORIGINAL SCULPTURE An original David Winter Cottage is always sculpted using standard artists' modelling wax, pale yellow in colour and a material ideal for the job — soft enough to be easily moulded but firm enough to retain the fine detail once it has been applied. David works in two stages: 1) making plain blocks of wax in a variety of shapes and combining them to create a satisfactory form for the piece; 2) adding the detail. Surprisingly 'blocking up' is the more time consuming (and enjoyable) of the two and he may deliberate over and modify a piece for quite some time until it is satisfactory. The detailing usually comes quickly. David always works from the top downwards to avoid smudging what he has already done. His tools include traditional sculpting and dental equipment, but mainly tools he has made himself over the years to cater for the specific needs of working on miniature cottages.

MOULDMAKING When he has completed a new model, David then hands it over to the Master Mouldmaking Department whose task it is to create a mould of the piece from which perfect copies can be made. To do so they must first make a copy of the piece in a stronger material than wax. They do so by placing the wax original under a container which has a hole in the top. Liquid silicon rubber is poured in through the hole until it has completely covered the wax. When the rubber has set the container is removed and the wax dug out of the solid rubber block. (David's original model is destroyed in the process.) Liquid resin is then poured in in place of the wax and when set can be removed to produce a perfect and very tough replica of David's original wax.

Using the resin 'master' the process is repeated to produce more resin copies which are in turn used to produce the silicon moulds needed by the Casting Department. The materials used (silicon rubber for moulds and resin for masters) are so compatible that none of David's fine detail is lost in the process.

(At this stage some of the resin pieces become colourways; pieces for test painting to originate a definitive colour scheme.)

CASTING/DEMOULDING In the Casting Department, the silicon rubber moulds are filled with liquid Crystacal, a fast setting and durable type of plaster which is again fine enough to retain the detail. The caster's two main enemies are distortion and pockets of air trapped in the mould. Distortion is prevented by placing the moulds (which are quite floppy) into a specially shaped outer casing; air pockets are avoided by fingering the inside of the mould (a messy job) and tapping the side of the casing to bring the air to the surface.

Once the Crystacal has set hard, a mould is gently removed by peeling it away from the piece. This is a delicate operation as both the piece and the mould can be easily damaged. Eventually when the piece has emerged safely the mould will be inside-out; if intact it can be used time and again to make more models.

The base of a David Winter Cottage always forms the opening in the mould through which the liquid Crystacal is poured. If you imagine then that a piece is always cast upside down with the base pointing upwards, this must always be the widest part of the model, otherwise the mould would be stretched and split during demoulding. David always sculpts his original with this important factor in mind.

FETTLING Using a scalpel, excess Crystacal, if any, is scraped away from the white unpainted model. This is primarily necessary at a 'shim', the point where two sections of rubber join together inside the mould to create an archway or tunnel.

DIPPING Crystacal is quite a porous material and a white piece must be dipped in a sealing solution of shellac and white polish prior to painting. If this is not done, the paint is absorbed into the Crystacal and becomes very dull.

PAINTING When the colours of a new Cottage have been decided upon, several identical pieces are painted by the Painting Master Originator and distributed to the workshops as guides for the painters. (For many years the Painting Master Originator was Audrey White; now Kerry Agar has assumed the responsibility.)

At one time John Hine Studios operated a network of homepainters as well as using painters in their own workshops, but all the work is currently undertaken in-house. Freedom for individual painters to interpret a piece to a certain degree is inevitable and

comparing painting variations is indeed part of the enjoyment of collecting David Winter Cottages. However, guidelines are much more stringent today than they were in the early 1980s when, in some cases, experimentation was encouraged.

Although the style has changed, the paints themselves have altered very little. The acrylic paints used on the heraldic plaques in 1979 were unsuitable for Cottages and powder paints mixed with water gave a lifeless appearance. It was David Winter who hit on the idea of mixing powder paints with methylated spirits and white polish, the formula that gives a slight sheen to the pieces but not a high gloss. It also makes the paint very fluid and allows it to flow into inaccessible corners and across expanses of tile or brick.

FINISHING When the overall painting is complete, the final details are added at the 'finishing' stage — metal accessories, special painting requirements (such as gold), baise and either a backstamp or the new barcoded disc. Last of all, each piece is boxed ready for dispatched to stores worldwide.

Colour Variations

In 1980 the Cottages were sparsely painted in soft, muted colours. Audrey White was using twelve basic colours and the simple painting style reflected the lack of fine detail on the first pieces David made. But as the detailing became more distinct and prominent, so colours became bolder, with greater tonal contrast, and the range of colours expanded. As the 80s progressed, feedback from the American market indicated a clear preference for brasher, brighter colours, which further encouraged a bold approach — and 'pale' and 'bright' versions of pieces have been a feature ever since.

Guidelines in the early 80s were less stringent, and in some cases homepainters were encouraged to interpret pieces in their own way — for example with The Village. Nowadays masters are supplied as a firm guide from which to work — copies of Kerry Agar's original. Even so, colour variations occur because each painter interprets what they see in a slightly different way, the end result being that collectors have an element of choice which would not be the case were David Winter Cottages not handmade and handpainted. Even if two pieces are painted in identical colours, one may be appear much bolder than the other due to the consistency of the paint mix. This also affects the amount of gloss on a piece.

The methylated spirits in the mix gradually evaporates as a painter works (especially during hot weather) and the paint thickens. This means that the proportion of shellac is greater and it is the natural sheen of shellac which gives a gloss effect. Paints must be topped up with fresh 'meths' to restore the right consistency.

Colour variations rarely make a difference to secondary market prices, but the quality of the painting may. Early Cottages are commonly 'brightened up' for a market which is now used to bolder colours, sometimes to the detriment of the piece.

Variations In Detail

Modifications and reworkings of pieces are listed in detail under the individual sections of this book. They apply primarily to early pieces which were usually modified for one of two reasons: 1) to make demoulding pieces easier and thus minimise wastage of time and raw materials (and therefore money) in the workshops; 2) to restore detail to a piece lost through wear and tear in the moulds — a problem which improved technology has now eradicated.

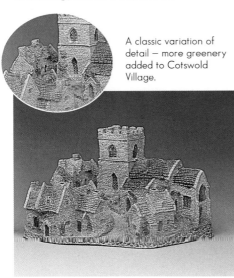

A classic variation of detail — more greenery added to Cotswold Village.

There are other reasons. Mould distortion was a problem on early David Winter Cottages; Dove Cottage, for example, may vary in shape from one piece to another. Mould shrinkage affected other pieces, the best example being Single Oast which shrank by half-an-inch all round before being restored to its original size in 1985. Occasionally David may make a change for aesthetic reasons, such as the addition of ropes weighted with stones to Crofters Cottage to create Scottish Crofters.

Other variations are listed further on in this section under 'Recognising Early Pieces'.

Name Variations

The spelling of names of pieces on backstamps, boxes and in printed material sometimes vary, as in the case of Falstaff's

The West Country Collection
Tamar Cottage TM
by David Winter TM
© 1986 David Winter
Hand made and hand painted in the Studios & Workshops of John Hind Ltd.
Hampshire, Great Britain

It's not just the cottage names that vary. Here the company name receives an accidental change!

Manor. They are interesting to note though rarely affect the value of a piece. A name change, on the other hand, may do so. Audrey's Tea Shop and Audrey's Tea Room are identical apart from the name on the backstamp, yet a 'Shop' is rarer and more valuable than a 'Room'.

The Hogs Head Tavern is often called Hogs Head Beer House. This may be connected to a series of alternative names considered in the mid-80s as more suitable for the American market but not adopted: The Toll House, Artisans Terrace (Craftsmen's Cottages), The Old Priory (Blackfriars Grange), The Manor (probably Shirehall), Village Stores (The Village Shop), The Farmhouse (Yeoman's Farmhouse), The Thatches (Meadowbank Cottages), The Village Church (St. George's Church).

Edition Sizes

With a few exceptions, the production runs of most David Winter Cottages are unknown. Popular pieces such as The Bothy, The Bakehouse and Rose Cottage have clearly been made in large quantities over a period of more than a decade and are amongst the most commonly found in collector's homes. Others — Double Oast and Sabrina's Cottage, for example — were available for a short time only, did not sell particularly well and are now very rare, as their secondary market prices reflect. But in all these cases, the exact quantities are a matter for speculation. When edition sizes are known they are quoted in this book.

The exceptions include pieces such as Wintershill (Jim'll Fix It), a charity piece produced in an edition of just 250 in 1988, and the recent prestige pieces Mad Baron Fourthrite's Folly (18,854) and Horatio Pernickety's Amorous Intent (9,990).

Guild pieces tend to have low edition sizes and the quantities made are determined by Guild membership numbers. The redemption pieces are a particularly good investment as not all Guild members chose to order them and the edition sizes are lower than the complementary gift pieces.

When long standing pieces retire such as The Winemerchant, Single Oast and Tudor Manor House, they are slow to increase in value on the secondary market. In these cases, it is the early mould versions and pieces with early labels which fetch the best prices.

Backstamps

The backstamps and labels on David Winter Cottages are an interesting study in themselves. They also provide useful information in determining the date when pieces were produced at John Hine Studios. The very first Cottages produced had neither baise nor backstamp and labels, and baise alone was added a little later. A number of customers of the first stockist of David Winter Cottages — David Windsor's in Guildford — were contacted whilst researching this book. Pieces purchased from there in 1980 and 1981 (The Mill House, Tythe Barn, Triple Oast, Castle Keep) which have remained in the original owners' possession ever since, were found to be

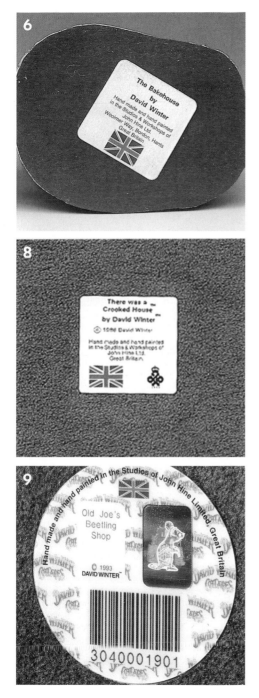

baised but without any backstamp or label. In some cases, the owners didn't know the name of the pieces that had been on their shelves for thirteen years!

1 *1980* The first type of base identification of any kind was a white oblong with black border, the words *Produced by a member of The Guild of Master Craftsmen* and the Guild of Master craftsmen's logo. The name of the piece and David's name were not included.

2 *1980-83* Plain oblong quoting the name of the piece, David's name and identifying him as a Member of the Guild of Master Craftsmen.

3 *1981-83* Diamond-shaped text with the name of the piece encircled by text similar to Type 2.

4 *1982-84* Plain, oblong (or square) with piece name, David's name and *Made and Hand Painted in Great Britain.*

5 *1985-87* Square with piece name, David's name plus a) the copyright symbol © and year c) a colour representation of the Union Jack and b) a reference for the first time to the manufacturer — *Hand made and hand painted in the Studios and Workshops of John Hine Ltd., Hendon Road, Bordon, Hants, Great Britain* .

6 *1985-88* Identical to Type 4 but with the new workshop address: *Woolmer Way, Bordon, Hants. Great Britain* .

7 *1985-88* Identical to Type 4 but with a) the addition of Trade Mark identification (TM) and b) a simplified address in two variations: *Hampshire, Great Britain* or just *Great Britain* .

8 *1988-93* The standard backstamp for this period: square (or slightly oblong) with piece name, David's name, TM symbol, © symbol, text *Hand made and hand painted in the Studios and Workshops of John Hine Ltd., Hampshire, Great Britain* (*Hampshire* was gradually omitted as production moved more and more to Wrexham, North Wales) PLUS the addition of the Queen's Award for Export Achievement logo. If part of a collection, the name appears above the piece name (e.g. The Midland Collection).

9 *1993-* A circular plastic disc inset into the base of the piece, with a background design featuring *David Winter Cottage* logos. Superimposed are: a) a Union Jack; b) a panel with the piece name, David's name, © symbol and date; c) a hologram of the

Studios and Workshops of John Hine Limited logo and a mouse; d) a barcode and number unique to the individual piece; e) the wording *Hand made and hand painted in the Studios of John Hine Limited, Great Britain.* (The disc was introduced for greater authenticity and to subdue the grey market.)

SOME SPECIALS AND EXCEPTIONS

There are exceptions and variations to these basic types:

* Special Christmas pieces with a more graphic design for the piece name, plus David's signature.

* Sometimes Guild pieces have a thin black border around the backstamp.

* British Traditions pieces have an entirely different design — oblong, bordered, featuring all the conventional information (apart from the year) plus © JHL and the specific month of the British Tradition. The Union Jack and Queen's Award logo are replaced by an illustration of Britannia (female warrior) holding a Union Jack shield.

* Birthstone Wishing Well had twelve variations each with the text and flower illustration relevant to a month of the year - has Union Jack but no Queens Award logo. In the address *Hampshire* is back.

* Welsh Collection pieces feature an illustration of a red dragon in place of the Union Jack and Queen's Award logo (which was phased out during 1993) plus additional text below the address: *Made in Wales - Gwyneud yng Nghymru .*

* Arches Thrice includes the wording: *available exclusively during David Winter's North American Tour April/May 1993.*

* The Castle Cottage of Warwick has special text commemorating CARNIVAL '93 plus the Bear and Ragged Staff (emblem of Warwick) in brown.

Boxes and Packaging

BOXES

March 1980 - March 1981 Cottages were sold unboxed and wrapped in tissue paper.

April 1981 - March 1985 Plain brown boxes, the type still used today for larger pieces such as The Parsonage.

March 1985 - October 1986 Mottled brownish green boxes introduced at certain sizes. If a particular size was not available, plain white boxes were used, and still are for smaller and medium-sized pieces.

October 1986 - Introduction of the familiar design of village characters and scenes against a variety of colour tinted backgrounds — yellow, red and blue.

Special Boxes Since A Christmas Carol in 1989, each special Christmas pieces have come in a special illustrated box — so too have the Christmas Ornaments. Brian Lee's artwork for the 1993 Christmas piece, Old Joe's Beetling Shop, was particularly impressive. Other prestige pieces have also had customised boxes — CASTLE IN THE AIR, Mad Baron Fourthrite's Folly and Horatio Pernickety's Amorous Intent.

Never throw the boxes away. They are extremely valuable when considering resale of pieces.

PACKING

The Cottages are protected inside the box in several ways:

1 Layers of bubble-wrap.

2 Bubble-wrap plus polystyrene chunks (called 'snow').

3 Two specially moulded foam cushions made in-house at John Hine Studios.

Certificates Of Authenticity

These were introduced in 1984 and are to be found inside the box with every piece. Replacements were freely available at one time from John Hine Studios. However, they are now more reluctant to supply them. So keep them safe and if you are purchasing on the secondary market, always ask the vendor for the certificate.

Originally the wording on the Certificates was as follows:

We hereby certify that this piece is an authentic David Winter Cottage, hand-made and hand-painted at the Studios and Workshops of John Hine Limited, Woolmer Way, Bordon, Hampshire, England, under the personal supervision of David Winter and John Hine.

The wording was later changed when it was practically impossible for the 'personal supervision' to continue:

We hereby certify that this piece is an authentic David Winter Cottage, hand-made and hand-painted at the Studios and Workshops of John Hine Limited, Woolmer Way, Bordon, Hampshire, England, under the guidance of David Winter and John Hine.

For most Cottages the Certificate includes a short piece of text about the piece. There are also special Certificates for certain pieces, such as Guild redemption items and the Christmas 'collection'.

Recognising Early Pieces

There is a far greater awareness amongst collectors today of the difference between early and late versions of the same piece, and this is being reflected in secondary market prices. Rose Cottage, for example, has been in production at John Hine Studios for more than thirteen years and has changed substantially. You can still purchase a Rose Cottage in stores in 1994, but the models made in 1980 and 1981 are worth more. Other pieces which fall into this category are Tudor Manor House, The Winemerchant, Market Street, Single and Triple Oast.

So be aware of the characteristics of early versions. Examples are indicated in brackets:

Chimneys - small and squat, not protruding above roof level. Mouldmaking technology was fairly basic in the 'coalshed days' and precluded the exposed chimney stacks of later versions (The Winemerchant, Tudor Manor House).

Foliage and flowers - absent on early pieces. Flowers were not added as a rule until 1982 — Brookside Hamlet onwards — nor was foliage until about the same time. From then onwards it has become more and more evident, with early pieces being restyled to include both (Single Oast, Tudor Manor House). Extra foliage is used as a useful means of disguising damage and distortion in moulds. It grows up walls on later pieces (Ebenezer Scrooge's Counting House) and forms arches on others (Cotswold Village, The Village).

Base Markings - The familiar standard base mark (example — © DAVID WINTER 1994) is absent from most early pieces and was frequently added at a later stage. David went through a spate of adapting the moulds of many pieces in about 1983 to include his signature, the date and © copyright symbol, had they been omitted from the original (Market Street). Some had just the signature to which he added the date and © symbol (Ivy Cottage, Single Oast).

Name Plaques - Early pieces frequently had a plaque sculpted to the side of the base indicating the name of the piece (Rose Cottage, Tudor Manor House). They are missing from later and restyled versions of pieces.

Other Considerations - Detail generally less defined, especially tiles, brickwork and beams (Market Street, Little Market). Sparsely painted in mute tones. See also the section on Backstamps.

For specific details of individual pieces see text in Section Two and comparison photographs in Section Three.

The Secondary Market

When John Hine Studios retire a David Winter Cottage, production ceases and, once existing stocks have been sold, the piece will no longer be available from their stockists (the primary market). It then becomes classified as a 'limited edition' item, invariably increases in value beyond its issue price and thus becomes highly collectable. The only way to purchase the piece from then onwards is from someone who already owns one, be they a collector or dealer. This additional buying and selling is referred to as the 'secondary market'.

Although David Winter Cottages have been retired since the very beginning of their short history, the secondary market did not begin in all seriousness until the second half of the 1980s and can be traced specifically to the retirement of Tythe Barn in 1986. This created waves amongst the rapidly increasing number of avid collectors who feared they had missed out on a popular piece. It was then that the demand for early pieces came sharply into focus and that every future retirement began to created a flurry of activity in within collecting fraternity.

In the ensuing years the secondary market has developed with remarkable momentum. In 1991 an authorised stockist in Illinois, USA, described David Winter Cottages as having "taken the country by storm," with everyone wanting retired pieces. Regular additional retirements have since extended the list of pieces which have long outstripped their issue price to eighty or more, and what goes on with David Winter Cottages has become the pastime of a small army of pundits. Like any market, prices are apt to fluctuate according to supply and demand, and the reasons can be quite sophisticated. Nevertheless it should be remembered that no matter what opinions may be expressed and predictions made, true market values are primarily set by people buying and selling.

It should be pointed out that such dealing is carried out independently of John Hine Studios who, as the manufacturers, have always (rightly) maintained a policy of non-involvement in the secondary market.

National Trends

By far the greatest amount of secondary market activity takes place in North America, where Canada's small but enthusiastic group of collectors are swamped in sheer volume by the USA at a ratio of 20 to 1 (using 1993 Guild membership numbers as a guideline). Due to the size of the American market, recently retired pieces are more commonly available on the secondary market there than in the UK, whereas earlier pieces, some of which were not sold outside the UK on the primary market, are proportionately much rarer. Special Guild pieces, too, have been exported in greater numbers to North America than were sold on the domestic UK market.

By the same token there are nine North American for every British collector. Although a severe economic recession has not necessarily curtailed collectors' enthusiasm for David Winter Cottages in Britain (1993 UK Guild membership reached an all time high), it has prevented them from paying high prices for pieces and indeed obliged some to sell when they would prefer to buy. Nevertheless on the whole the belief in the long term investment potential of collectables has given the pieces a certain 'recession-proof' credibility.

Trans-Atlantic dealing is commonplace on the secondary market and fluctuations in the exchange rate can make a considerable difference to the comparative values of pieces. A sterling/dollar parity (US$1 = UK£1), for example, would have UK dealers rubbing their hands with glee when selling to American collectors, but it would also make sales from the US to the UK inordinately expensive. In contrast, a $2 = £1 situation would force prices up in the US if pieces were being purchased from the UK. Exchange rates are worth keeping an eye on.

David Winter Cottages are very popular amongst US military personnel, many of who start collecting whilst posted to the UK and central Europe. As a result, there is a healthy interest in the secondary market on military bases, in Germany especially. Prices are usually quoted in US dollars and are marginally higher than US equivalents.

In recent years Australia has spawned an increased number of collectors, one or two who have been very active in developing the secondary market and generating contacts worldwide. Prices (both current and retired) 'down under' tend to be high due to a combination of shipping charges and import duty.

Where Should I Buy & How Much Should I Pay

Current Pieces John Hine Studios recommend purchasing only from their authorised stockists. If you give them a ring they will happily supply you with details of stores in your area. Authorised stockists provide quality of service, back up, accurate information and availability of all product, including Guild pieces; not to mention the advantages which may materialise from becoming a regular and valued customer.

David Winter Cottages can also be found in unauthorised outlets (mainly in North America) which have been supplied indirectly from authorised stockists in Europe — grey marketeering, as it is known. Prices are generally cheaper and seemingly more attractive. But beware — purchasing from them can be a false economy. Substantially discounted issue prices undermine the inherent value of the pieces and retard their value as collectables (which in the long term far outweighs the initial saving of a few pounds or dollars).

Grey marketeering is a difficult problem to tackle from John Hine Studios' point of view. Proving which European stockists are supplying the USA is the first hurdle to overcome; the second is to turn down sales (bearing in mind the severity of the UK recession) in order to stabilise future markets. However, since the company became primarily American owned in December 1993, there is bound to be fresh impetus to restore the market to authorised stockists only . . . and a good thing, too.

Retired Pieces There are many dealers worldwide who now specialise in the buying and selling of discontinued Cottages, including collectors who have converted their pastime into a source of income. They advertise regularly in magazines, newspapers, collectors club newsletters and periodicals, many of which are listed in Section Three. In the UK stockists in remote spots still occasionally have retired pieces or early mould versions on their shelves and a spot of detective work does not go amiss. Car boot sales and bric-a-brac shops are also worth visiting as rare early David Winters crop up from time to time for just a few pounds — if luck is with you.

Collectors selling their pieces should bear in mind that a dealer will offer a lower price than those quoted in this book in order to make a profit by reselling them. Just how much lower various enormously. 40% would be a fair average, but this will fluctuate depending on prevailing circumstances; the number of pieces being sold, their condition, demand for particular pieces at the time.

Exchanges between collectors adhere more to the full market value as a profit margin is not necessarily a prerequisite. Swapping pieces of equivalent value is common, and the idea of no money changing hands appeals to those collectors who prefer to think of David Winter Cottages in purely aesthetic terms.

However, there is no denying the monetary value of the Cottages which demand has created, and dealers are there to provide pieces for collectors who want them. If their price does not match your budget . . . negotiate!

Signed Pieces

David Winter's signature on the base of a piece will undoubtedly increase its inherent value; the Cottage has been in contact with the man who sculpted it and has his personal touch. The increase in monetary value that a signature gives is clearly there, but extremely difficult to quantify. It should be regarded as a significant 'selling point' and reason for a vendor to be looking for a higher price.

Signed pieces are more common nowadays than in the 1980s as David has devoted more time to personal appearances and signing sessions in the last three or four years. Nevertheless they are still a drop in the ocean compared to the number that he hasn't personalised, and the signature is significant. A signed piece is branded with an indelible guarantee of authenticity which words on a slip of paper cannot equal.

Carnival '93

John Hine Studios launched what promises to be a series of regular annual events in October 1993 with CARNIVAL '93 — a two day promotion held at Warwick Castle. From the collecting point of view, the biggest attraction was a special piece — The Castle Cottage of Warwick — sculpted by David Winter exclusively for the event and

available only to ticket holders in person. Becoming a limited edition so rapidly (and a low edition at that) has made the piece an excellent investment for collectors and secondary market dealers alike, and future CARNIVALS or similar promotions should be watched with great interest.

Counterfeits

In the early 1990s a number of counterfeit David Winter Cottages were known to be in circulation on the secondary market. However, the quantities were very small indeed and the sources were rapidly tracked down and eradicated by John Hine Studios. The experience has made collectors and dealers more vigilant and thus reduced the likelihood of a recurrence.

A few words of advice:
1   Compare the piece with the pictures in this and other books, or in Cottage Country magazine. Look particularly for loss of fine detail such as tiles and bricks.
2   Be aware of the paint. Early pieces were painted in very mute colours, and a brightly coloured Mill House or Forge, for instance, would be unusual (though not unheard of; collectors do sometimes have early pieces repainted). Smell the piece. If your nose detects the methylated spirits and white polish, then it may have been repainted since the early 1980s.
3   Peel away a corner of the baise and look at the base. Crystacal dulls with age, and a bright, clean white base may be inconsistent with a piece made more than a decade ago. The baise itself will look aged if it is original, though new baise is sometimes added to pieces by dealers for cosmetic effect.
4   Study the backstamp. The genuine article look their age and are very difficult to counterfeit. They can be photocopied of course, so look at the paper, too. The absence of a backstamp from a very early piece is not necessarily significant, though worthy of further inspection of the piece.
5   Don't be over suspicious. Counterfeiting is difficult, dangerous and extremely rare. Above all, ask yourself if the value of the piece you are studying is worth someone going to all that trouble.
6   The ultimate guarantee of authenticity is David Winter's signature on the base of a piece.

Cleaning & Care

The safest and cleanest place for a David Winter Cottage is in its box. But if collectors insist on displaying them in their homes, here are a few suggestions on how to take care of them:
1   A *dry* cloth can be used for removing dust from large surface areas such as roofs and walls. For getting into the nooks and crannies use a dry, soft paint brush, toothbrush, cosmetic brush or photographer's lens brush. Always brush with the line of tiles, bricks etc.
3   Alternatively try a hairdryer, which has the advantage of never touching the piece.
2   NEVER use a wet cloth or immerse David Winter Cottages in water. Not only will dampness damage the paintwork but the piece itself may begin to disintegrate.
3   Keep your Cottages out of direct sunlight wherever possible.
4   Do not pick pieces up by the chimney or other delicate feature.
5   Never try repairing your own pieces with superglue or touching up chips with felt tip pens. Get someone who knows what they are doing to repair them for you.
6   Make sure display shelves can take the weight. It's easy to underestimate just how heavy a growing collection can become, especially with the acquisition of larger pieces such as The Parsonage and The Old Distillery.
7   Avoid living in areas where earthquakes, civil unrest and clumsy people occur!

Section Two

Secondary Market Price Guide

Listed here are the original issue prices, final retail prices (prior to retirement) and current valuations of all retired David Winter Cottages. Prices which originally included pence/cents have been rounded up to the nearest pound/dollar. It must be stressed that the current valuations quoted are intended as a guide only. The secondary market is an ever-fluctuating beast! A piece is only worth what a buyer is willing to pay and a seller is willing to accept.

The best prices are paid for well cast and well painted pieces in perfect condition, with their original box and certificate of authenticity. David Winter's signature on the base of a piece is also worthy of a higher valuation.

Collectors selling to dealers should be prepared to deduct anything from 10% to 50% from the prices quoted. 40% is probably an acceptable working average.

Issue prices are based on original price lists in John Hine Studios' archives. In the UK they date back to the very first sale in March 1980, and in North America to 1985.

N/A (Not Applicable or Not Available) refers primarily to pieces which were never available on the primary market in that particular currency.

Current valuations have been compiled from extensive surveying of the market between January and April 1994.

Despite its relatively short history, the secondary market in David Winter Cottages has come of age and collectors and dealers know their market. Bargains are harder to come by, and it is worth bearing in mind that ultimately a 'bargain' is not a piece that is purchased for less than it is worth — it is a piece that has been purchased for less than you were prepared to pay.

NAME	ISSUE PRICE		FINAL PRICE		CURRENT PRICE	
	UK £	US $	UK £	US $	UK £	US $
ANNE HATHAWAY'S COTTAGE (Tiny)	2	N/A	3	N/A	300-400	600-1200
ARCHES THRICE	N/A	150	N/A	150	175-200	150-300
AUDREY'S TEA ROOM	40	90	40	90	100-150	120-200
(With Tea Shop backstamp)	40	90	40	90	200-250	300-400
THE ALMS HOUSES	22	60	25	71	250-400	450-650
THE BEEKEEPER'S	34	65	34	65	45-70	80-100
BIRTHSTONE WISHING WELL	25	55	25	55	30-35	40-50
BLACK BESS INN	25	60	25	60	140-200	175-300
BLACKSMITH'S COTTAGE	6	22	8	27	150-250	450-500

NAME	ISSUE PRICE		FINAL PRICE		CURRENT PRICE	
	UK £	US $	UK £	US $	UK £	US $
BOOKENDS						
(The Printers/The Bookbinders)	50	120	55	138	50-60	140-150
BOTTLE KILN	28	78	45	90	50-75	100-125
BROOKSIDE HAMLET	23	75	48	97	50-100	100-200
THE CANDLEMAKER'S	34	65	34	65	50-70	85-125
THE CASTLE COTTAGE OF WARWICK	100	N/A	100	N/A	200-300	350-500
CASTLE GATE	60	130	114	230	125-200	200-300
CASTLE KEEP	7	N/A	7	N/A	700-900	1500-2200
(with 'Guildford Castle' plaque)	7	N/A	7	N/A	1000-1100	2000+
CARTWRIGHT'S COTTAGE	35	45	35	45	70-125	75-200
THE CHAPEL	20	50	30	80	50-70	90-125
CHICHESTER CROSS	17	N/A	17	N/A	1500-2000	3300-3600
In perfect condition	17	N/A	17	N/A	2000-2500	4000+
In cold cast bronze	45	N/A	45	N/A	4500+	6000-7500
A CHRISTMAS CAROL	46	135	46	135	100-175	110-350
CHRISTMAS IN SCOTLAND						
AND HOGMANAY	46	100	46	100	100-200	125-225
THE COBBLER	15	40	15	40	50-85	75-100
THE COACHING INN	36	165	50	165	1500-2000	3000-4500
THE COAL SHED	50	112	50	112	150-200	150-300
THE COOPER'S COTTAGE	20	60	36	80	35-70	85-125
CORNISH COTTAGE	8	30	11	35	400-600	900-1450
CORNISH TIN MINE	7	22	9	26	50-100	75-125

NAME	ISSUE PRICE		FINAL PRICE		CURRENT PRICE	
	UK £	US $	UK £	US $	UK £	US $
COTSWOLD FARMHOUSE (Tiny)	2	N/A	3	N/A	300-400	600-1200
COTSWOLD VILLAGE	20	60	44	86	60-100	75-125
THE COTTON MILL	14	42	19	56	300-450	600-1000
CROFTER'S COTTAGE	17	51	19	51	70-100	75-125
CROWN INN (Tiny)	2	N/A	3	N/A	300-400	600-1200
DIORAMA FOR CAMEOS						
(Lightly painted)	25	52	25	52	40-60	60-100
DOUBLE OAST	10	N/A	12	N/A	1600-2000	3500-4300
DOVE COTTAGE	8	60	12	60	700-900	1500-2300
THE DOWER HOUSE	6	22	12	32	15-30	40-65
EBENEZER SCROOGE'S						
COUNTING HOUSE	43	97	43	97	150-200	180-350
FAIRYTALE CASTLE						
Mould 1	40	115	Unknown		225-275	400-500
Mould 2	Unknown		60	136	190-250	225-300
FALSTAFF'S MANOR	115	242	140	360	300-400	350-450
THE FORGE	9	60	12	60	750-950	1800-2500
FRED'S HOME . . .	60	145	60	145	70-125	100-150
THE GRANGE	60	120	120	240	650-800	900-1600
THE HAYBARN	6	22	9	27	150-225	300-450
HERMIT'S HUMBLE HOME	32	87	40	95	180-225	250-400
HERTFORD COURT	30	00	60	124	65-100	110-175
HOME GUARD	46	105	46	105	150-200	150-250

NAME	ISSUE PRICE		FINAL PRICE		CURRENT PRICE	
	UK £	US $	UK £	US $	UK £	US $
HORATIO PERNICKETY'S						
AMOROUS INTENT	175	350	175	350	175-225	250-350
HOUSE OF THE MASTER MASON	32	75	40	88	200-250	250-400
HOUSE ON TOP	32	92	46	108	200-250	275-400
IRISH WATER MILL	0	0	0	0	35-50	50-80
(With Patrick's backstamp)	0	0	0	0	100-130	100-200
IVY COTTAGE	6	20	18	32	25-40	50-90
JOHN BENBOW'S FARM HOUSE	25	74	40	85	40-60	80-100
LITTLE FORGE	5	27	8	27	700-1000	1700-3400
LITTLE MARKET	9	27	24	52	25-40	50-100
LITTLE MILL						
Mould 1	5	N/A	5	N/A	1000-1350	1800-2300
Mould 2	Unknown		Unknown		800-1000	1400-1800
Mould 3	Unknown		8	40	650-750	1200-1400
MAD BARON FOURTHRITE'S FOLLY	150	275	150	275	150-190	175-325
MILL HOUSE						
Mould 1	8	N/A	8	N/A	1200-1450	2000-2800
Mould 2	8	50	14	N/A	850-1100	1600-2000
MINER'S COTTAGE	6	22	9	27	140-200	250-300
MISTER FEZZIWIG'S EMPORIUM	60	135	60	135	90-125	100-175
MOORLAND COTTAGE	6	22	9	27	150-200	250-350
THE OLD CURIOSITY SHOP						
Moulds 1,2,3,4 (with windows)	10	40	10	40	650-1000	1200-1600

NAME	ISSUE PRICE		FINAL PRICE		CURRENT PRICE	
	UK £	US $	UK £	US $	UK £	US $
Mould 5 (without windows)	12	40	12	40	1000-1200	1600-2000
THE OLD DISTILLERY	95	270	264	550	265-300	400-600
OLD JOE'S BEETLING SHOP	75	175	75	175	75-125	175-200
ON THE RIVERBANK	0	0	0	0	25-50	50-80
ONLY A SPAN APART	38	80	38	80	40-50	75-100
ORCHARD COTTAGE	42	91	60	115	60-100	100-150
THE PAVILION	23	52	23	52	150-200	150-300
PERSHORE MILL	0	0	0	0	50-100	75-115
PILGRIM'S REST	12	40	36	84	50-60	80-125
THE PLUCKED DUCKS	0	0	0	0	70-90	75-135
PLUM COTTAGE	40	50	50	90	160-250	200-300
THE POTTERY	15	40	15	40	50-75	75-100
PROVENCAL ONE	8	N/A	N/A	N/A	2500-4500	7500+
PROVENCAL TWO	8	N/A	N/A	N/A	7000+	Unknown
PROVENCAL A (Tiny)	3	N/A	N/A	N/A	700-800	1500-2000
PROVENCAL B (Tiny)	3	N/A	N/A	N/A	700-800	1500-2000
QUAYSIDE	9	52	12	60	700-900	1600-2500
QUEEN ELIZABETH SLEPT HERE	70	183	70	183	200-375	300-500
ROBIN HOOD'S HIDEAWAY	18	54	18	54	250-375	350-550
SABRINA'S COTTAGE	6	N/A	6	N/A	900-1200	1900-2500
ST NICHOLAS' CHURCH (Tiny)	2	N/A	3	N/A	300-400	600-1200
ST PAUL'S CATHEDRAL	9	N/A	N/A	N/A	750-1000	1700-2500
SCROOGE'S SCHOOL	75	100	75	100	75-125	150-200

NAME	ISSUE PRICE		FINAL PRICE		CURRENT PRICE	
	UK £	US $	UK £	US $	UK £	US $
SECRET SHEBEEN	36	70	36	70	35-50	75-100
SINGLE OAST						
Mould 1	7	27	9	27	40-50	125-350
Mould 2	10	30	24	52	25-30	45-55
SNOW COTTAGE	25	65	54	115	65-85	90-125
SPINNER'S COTTAGE	9	27	24	40	30-60	45-75
SQUIRES HALL	37	92	66	130	80-110	100-150
STREET SCENE (Bas Relief Plaque)	0	0	0	0	100-200	150-230
SUFFOLK HOUSE						
Pink	22	49	25	58	60-80	80-100
White	22	49	25	58	80-100	100-130
SULGRAVE MANOR (Tiny)	2	N/A	3	N/A	300-400	600-1200
SWAN UPPING COTTAGE	35	59	35	59	35-50	70-80
THAMESIDE	40	79	40	79	35-50	70-80
THREE DUCKS INN	8	N/A	15	N/A	750-1000	1500-2500
TOLLKEEPER'S COTTAGE	30	75	60	140	65-85	100-150
TOMFOOL'S COTTAGE	35	100	35	100	75-125	100-150
TUDOR MANOR HOUSE						
Mould 1	6	47	Unknown		350-450	500-600
Mould 2	6	47	Unknown		250-275	200-250
Mould 3	Unknown		36	84	60-100	90-200
TYTHE BARN						
Mould 1	11	39	11	39	800-1000	1800-2600

NAME	ISSUE PRICE		FINAL PRICE		CURRENT PRICE	
	UK £	US $	UK £	US $	UK £	US $
Mould 2	11	39	16	39	650-800	1500-2400
VILLAGE SCENE						
(Point of Sale)	0	0	0	0	130-175	250-450
(Guild Piece)	0	0	0	0	125-150	250-400
THE WINEMERCHANT						
Mould 1	9	27	Unknown		150-195	200+
Mould 2	Unknown		24	52	40-50	50-75
WINTERSHILL (Jim'll Fix It)	200	375	200	375	1500-1750	2500-3500
W. SHAKESPEARE'S BIRTHPLACE						
(Large)	20	60	24	60	700-1000	1200-1600
(Tiny Series)	2	N/A	3	N/A	300-400	600-1200
WILL-'O-THE-WISP	55	120	55	120	150-200	150-200
WOODCUTTERS COTTAGE	33	87	42	103	200-275	250-400
CHRISTMAS ORNAMENTS						
(Based on sculptures by David Winter)						
(1991 Set of 4)	24	60	24	60	40-65	60-80
(1992 Set of 4)	30	60	30	60	25-50	60
(1993 Set of 4)	30	60	30	60	25-40	60

NAME	ISSUE PRICE		FINAL PRICE		CURRENT PRICE	
	UK £	US $	UK £	US $	UK £	US $

Retired Pieces

These are pieces sculpted by David Winter which have been marketed commercially and withdrawn prior to spring 1994. The information given is based on examples of pieces which are known to exist from firsthand or reliable secondhand experience. However, details such as base markings are unlikely to be definitive as speculation has for the most part been avoided. The term Mould 1, 2 , 3 etc. is used to determine variations of a piece when they involve a specific modification, but not if changes were gradual over a period of time. New variations frequently come to light. For example, the reference to 'Dove Cottage' having a name plaque was included here only following the receipt of a photograph from a collector in the USA as proof. The expression N/A (Not Available) is used in the dollars price listings if the piece was retired from the primary market prior to availability in North America.

THE ALMS HOUSES

Early pieces (pre-1984) have deeper gutters and the stone walls are not as sturdy as on later models. It is common for one or more of the delicate spheres flanking the gables to be missing, to have been reattached or even replaced with a substitute. There is a marked similarity between the form of this piece and the frontage of the Hogs Back Hotel, near Farnham in Surrey, not far from David's home village — though David claims no conscious link.

SCULPTED: 1983
LOCATION: Faith Winter's Studio
RELEASED: 1983 RETIRED: 1987
SIZE: Width: 7" Depth: 4 ³/₈" Height: 4 ¹/₄"
MARKINGS: © DAVID WINTER 1983
ISSUE PRICE: £22 $60

33

AUDREY'S TEA ROOM/SHOP

SCULPTED: 1991
LOCATION: Home Studio
RELEASED: Jan/Feb 1992
RETIRED: March 1992
SIZE: Width: 3 ⁵/₈" Depth: 3 ¹/₄" Height: 5 ¹/₂"
MARKINGS: © DAVID WINTER 1991
ISSUE PRICE: £39.95 $90

Named as a tribute to Audrey White, the first painter of David Winter Cottages, who retired in September 1991 from her bench at Eggars Hill after twelve years of working with David Winter and John Hine. The piece was available for a short time only and was retired suddenly in March 1992. Sadly Audrey herself died four months later. It would seem that a considerable number were made — more than first imagined — and Audrey's Tea Room has never reached the high prices of The Grange, which was retired just as suddenly three years earlier. More collectable, however, are the small quantity (1,000 at a guess) released with the incorrect name on the box and backstamp — Audrey's Tea Shop. These were rushed out as stockists' samples before the name had been finalised. Apart from the name, the pieces are identical.

BLACKSMITH'S COTTAGE

SCULPTED: 1982
LOCATION: Hendon Road
RELEASED: 1982 RETIRED: 1986
SIZE: Width: 4 ¹/₈" Depth: 2" Height: 2"
MARKINGS: © DAVID WINTER 1983
ISSUE PRICE: £6 $22

Painting variations: some have black slate roofs with grey walls, others are all black. Technically the piece was retired in 1985, but stocks remained available from John Hine Studios to shops well into the following year.

BOOKENDS
(The Printers/The Bookbinders)

SCULPTED: 1989
LOCATION: Home Studio
RELEASED: 1991 RETIRED: 1994
SIZE: THE PRINTERS: Width: 3"
Depth: 2 3/4" Height: 4 3/4"
THE BOOKBINDERS: Width: 3 1/8"
Depth: 2 3/4" Height: 4 3/4"
MARKINGS: © D.W.C.1989
ISSUE PRICE: £50 $120

Although sculpted in 1989 (as a possible Guild exclusive), Bookends were not released until two years later. They were too lightweight to hold standard books in place, so John Hine withheld them whilst he penned twelve small books to complement the British Traditions collection. When displayed in the correct order the binders of the books cleverly form a picture featuring all the British Traditions pieces. Although the British Traditions books have been available for purchase individually, The Printers and The Bookbinders have only ever been sold as a pair.

BOTTLE KILN

SCULPTED: 1987
LOCATION: Home Studio
RELEASED: 1988
RETIRED: November 1991
SIZE: Width: 6 3/4" Depth: 4 3/4" Height: 4 1/2"
MARKINGS: © DAVID WINTER 1987
ISSUE PRICE: £28 $78

Launched initially as Bottle Kilns (there are three of them), but the 's' has somehow been lost along the way. For inspiration David visited the Gladstone Pottery Museum in Stoke-On-Trent, the very heart of bottle kiln country, and there are notable similarities between the two. Until its retirement, Bottle Kiln was part of the Midlands Collection.

BROOKSIDE HAMLET

SCULPTED: 1982
LOCATION: Hendon Road
RELEASED: 1982 RETIRED: April 1991
SIZE: Width: 7" Depth: 4 3/8" Height: 4 1/4"
MARKINGS: DAVID WINTER / © DAVID WINTER 1983
ISSUE PRICE: £23 $75

Brookside Hamlet was sculpted and released in 1982 without a date on the base marking. At a later stage the wrong year (1983) was added in error. This was the first piece sculpted by David in his new studio at the Hendon Road premises in Bordon. Early pieces lack water dripping from the water wheel, general foliage and in particular the greenery behind the wheel on the corner of the mill building. These items were added at various stages during 1984 and 1985, including greenery to fill in a recess adjacent to the front door of the building at top right. Consequently pieces produced during this period may vary in specific detail. From late 1985 onwards Brookside Hamlet remained unaltered. This piece was the feature of an illustrated short story entitled 'Brookside Hamlet — a Fable' in the small hardback Collectors Book produced by John Hine in the mid-'80s; a fascinating account of how the hamlet might have grown. Meanwhile back on the sculpture itself, look out for the very first mouse, a magnificent specimen!

CASTLE KEEP

(Guildford Castle)

SCULPTED: 1981
LOCATION: 19 Ash Street
RELEASED: 1981 RETIRED: 1982
SIZE: Width: 3 1/2" Depth: 3 3/4" Height: 2 3/4"
MARKINGS: © DAVID WINTER 1981
ISSUE PRICE: £22 $N/A

Mould 1 The very first shop to stock David Winter Cottages, *David Windsor's* in Guildford, suggested doing a model of Guildford Castle for them as an exclusive. David agreed and took reference pictures of the castle (only the central keep still stands) with his sister Alice in the foreground to help get the scale right. The piece was initially sold through David Windsor's under the name 'Guildford Castle' and was only changed to 'Castle Keep' when it was later made available to other stores. The original had a plaque sculpted onto one side with the inscription 'Guildford Castle.' *Mould 2* The inscription and the backstamp were then changed to read 'Castle Keep'. *Mould 3* Soon afterwards the plaque was removed altogether. On later pieces it will be noticed that some of the windows have been filled in. Examples of 'Guildford Castle' are very rare and highly collectable.

CASTLE GATE

SCULPTED: 1984
LOCATION: Hendon Road
RELEASED: 1984 RETIRED: February 1992
SIZE: Width: 7" Depth: 5" Height: 8 3/8"
MARKINGS: © DAVID WINTER 1984
ISSUE PRICE: £60 $130

Castle Gate remained standard throughout its seven year production run, although it changed in a fascinating way during the sculpting process. To give the effect he wanted, David first sculpted the castle part of the piece in a perfect state of repair — as if it had just been built. He then crumbled away parts of the facade to give the impression it had been ransacked. Finally he added the cottages approaching the gateway to give the impression that they have been built using stone from the castle ruin. In the pack of David Winter cards produced in 1984 (see Memorabilia) there is a photograph of David at work on his original wax and you can see the part of the castle which he later destroyed. He was pleased with the way Castle Gate turned out and it remains one of his favourite pieces.

THE CHAPEL

SCULPTED: 1984
LOCATION: 19 Ash Street
RELEASED: 1984 RETIRED: November 1992
SIZE: Width: 4 1/2" Depth: 3 5/8" Height: 5 3/4"
MARKINGS: © DAVID WINTER 1984
ISSUE PRICE: £20 $50

No production alterations were made and the piece remained standard. For some reason, David sculpted The Chapel on the kitchen table at 19 Ash Street!

CHICHESTER CROSS

SCULPTED: 1981
LOCATION: 19 Ash Street
RELEASED: 1981 RETIRED: 1981
SIZE: Width: 3 1/2" Depth: 3 1/2"
Height: 4 1/4" MARKINGS: None
ISSUE PRICE: £17 $N/A

This piece was not painted but dipped, originally in two colour variations — stone white and stone grey. A third choice was offered later — sandstone buff. *Good Ideas*, the David Winter stockist in Chichester, suggested doing a model of their town cross and David duly obliged. It was a difficult piece to sculpt, even more difficult to cast ("The mould looked ridiculous," David says), and very few pieces came out with all the pinnacles intact. Furthermore Crystacal proved too weak for such a complex piece and resin, a harder and more expensive material, had to be used which made the purchase price high. Not many were sold and possibly as few as a hundred were made in all. This a rare piece indeed and examples in perfect condition are virtually unheard of. Very collectable indeed.

THE COACHING INN

In the winter of 1980 John and David hired a unit at the Manor Farm Craft Centre for a short while to sell some cottages. Being just the two of them, John was out and about delivering cottages to stockists and so David remained at the Craft Centre to mind their own shop. It was during this short sojourn that he sculpted The Coaching Inn. (He nearly froze one day when he ran out of fuel for the heater; John remembers coming back at the end of the day and finding his colleague looking rather blue in colour!) A number of variations exist to The Coaching Inn. a) The pillars at the rear of the main front building were made of matchsticks on early models. They were later cast in Crystacal and glued into place and are thicker than the matchsticks. b) On a few early models the upstairs door of the thatched section was recessed into the wall, but this proved difficult to demould and so David filled in the hollow, leaving a plain ribbed effect. He later sculpted a door flush with the wall. c) Most models have an arched sign above the front courtyard entrance, with the inscription 'The White Hart.' But it was left off later models because the moulds had warped with use, the two buildings flanking the entrance had bowed apart and the sign no longer fitted into the larger space. Attempts to remedy the situation by gluing matchsticks to either wall to bridge the gap looked crude and were abandoned (although a few models were released like this). John Hine Studios used to provide replacement signs for collectors who felt they had missed out and wanted to have a go at attaching the sign themselves, but these are no longer available. Look closely at The Coaching Inn and you will see that David extracted two sections and adapted them into new Cottages: the thatched part became Rose Cottage and the main half-timbered building became Tudor Manor House.

SCULPTED: 1980
LOCATION: Manor Farm Craft Centre, Seale, Surrey
RELEASED: 1980 RETIRED: 1983
SIZE: Width: 11 ½" Depth: 7 ½" Height: 4 ½"
MARKINGS: © DAVID WINTER 1980
ISSUE PRICE: £36 $165

THE COOPER'S COTTAGE

O ne of few David Winter Cottages to feature pantiles on the roof. The others are House of the Master Mason and the Provencal pieces.

SCULPTED: 1985
LOCATION: 19 Ash Street
RELEASED: 1985 RETIRED: January 1993
SIZE: Width: 3" Depth: 3 ½" Height: 4 ½"
MARKINGS: © DAVID WINTER 1985
ISSUE PRICE: £20 $60

CORNISH COTTAGE

D avid began sculpting Cornish Cottage in July 1991 whilst on a short holiday in Cornwall, and he completed it on his return to 19 Ash Street. This is reflected in the customised backstamp which reads: *Sculpted in Cornwall by David Winter.* Whilst working on the piece he tried adding a wider base with rocks around the cottage; but he changed his mind and cut them away. In doing so he also sliced away his name from the base and forgot to put it back on — which is why Cornish Cottage has no markings! The brightly coloured front doors contrast starkly with the overall greyness of the cottage walls and roof — a common characteristic of real Cornish cottages. Some models are painted with darker walls, almost the colour of the roof. For years Cornish Cottage has been listed as a 1982 piece, but this is incorrect; it was sculpted in 1981. The piece was retired prior to the launch of the West Country Collection.

SCULPTED: 1981
LOCATION: Cornwall and 19 Ash Street
RELEASED: 1981 RETIRED: 1986
SIZE: Width: 5 ⅜" Depth: 2 ¾" Height: 2 ¾"
MARKINGS: None
ISSUE PRICE: £8 $30

CORNISH TIN MINE

SCULPTED: 1983
LOCATION: Home Studio
RELEASED: 1983 RETIRED: January 1989
SIZE: Width: 3 ¼" Depth: 2 ½" Height: 5 ¼"
MARKINGS: © DAVID WINTER 1983
ISSUE PRICE: £7 $22

Later models have more foliage than earlier ones — along the join between the mill and the chimney stack. This was added to provide strength in the mould. When the West Country Collection was being planned in 1987 it was decided to remodel Cornish Tin Mine slightly and to relaunch as part of the new collection. But David's modifications were so extensive that version 2 was renamed Cornish Engine House and classified as a new piece. (A similar thing happened with Cotton Mill.) The original and remodelled version were available concurrently until January 1989 when John Hine Studios' stocks of Cotton Mill had gone.

COTSWOLD VILLAGE

Cotswold Village was designed by David with photography in mind — low and openly spaced at the front and high at the back, so that a camera would catch as much detail as possible. Demoulding Cotswold Village proved tricky at first and the following modifications were made at various stages during the first year of production: a) Foliage arches added in two places; at the very back, between the side of the church and the adjacent cottage, and on the left side, at the end of an alleyway. b) On the right side, the space between the church and the cottage next to it was filled with greenery. c) Foliage was added in various places on the church walls and also spread onto the roof above the porch. d) Foliage added behind the two gravestones in front of the church tower. e) The overhang of the church porch was shortened.

SCULPTED: 1982
LOCATION: Hendon Road
RELEASED: 1982 RETIRED: 1990
SIZE: Width: 6 ¾" Depth: 4 ½" Height: 3 ⅝"
MARKINGS: © DAVID WINTER 1982
ISSUE PRICE: £20 $60

THE COTTON MILL

The foliage rising for about three inches between the mill building and chimney stack is missing on models produced during the first year of production. This was added in 1984 to add strength in the mould. As with Cornish Tin Mine, David intended remodelling The Cotton Mill slightly to be relaunched with a new collection — the Midland Collection. But his alterations turned out to be extensive and so the piece was renamed Derbyshire Cotton Mill and classified as a new piece. Both versions were available concurrently until January 1989 when John Hine Studios' stocks of The Cotton Mill had been sold.

SCULPTED: 1983
LOCATION: Hendon Road
RELEASED: 1983 RETIRED: January 1989
SIZE: Width: 4 ³/₈" Depth: 3 ³/₈" Height: 9 ¹/₈"
MARKINGS: © DAVID WINTER 1983
ISSUE PRICE: £14 $42

CROFTERS COTTAGE

An early version of Scottish Crofters and identical to it apart from the lack of ropes on the roof weighted down with stones. The alteration was made and the name changed when the piece was relaunched as part of the Scottish Collection in 1988. The two versions were available concurrently until at least the middle of 1989 when stocks of the original had all been sold.

SCULPTED: 1986
LOCATION: 19 Ash Street
RELEASED: 1986 RETIRED: July 1989
SIZE: Width: 5" Depth: 3 ¹/₂" Height: 4 ³/₄"
MARKINGS: © DAVID WINTER 1986
ISSUE PRICE: £17 $51

DOUBLE OAST

SCULPTED: 1981
LOCATION: 19 Ash Street
RELEASED: 1981 RETIRED: 1982
SIZE: Width: 5 ½" Depth: 4 ⅝" Height: 5 ⅜"
MARKINGS: DAVID WINTER
ISSUE PRICE: £10 $N/A

In 1981 David sculpted a set of three pieces — Single Oast, Double Oast and Triple Oast — at the suggestion of one of their stockists in Kent, where oast houses abound. But sales of Double Oast were poor as people chose either the small or large rather than the middle-sized piece, and in less than a year it had been withdrawn. Nowadays it is Double Oast that collectors dream of owning — a rare and much sought-after piece. Examples that do appear on the secondary market from time to time demonstrate how all three Oasts were designed and painted originally — no foliage, fences or hop poles on the ground, with grey rather than reddish brown roofs.

DOVE COTTAGE

Thought until recently to be one of the few David Winter Cottages without any base markings (signature or date). But an example came to light in 1993 with the base marking 'DOVE COTTAGE © DAVID WINTER'. Comparison of more than one model may highlight slight variations due to the mould distortion which regularly affected early pieces. Examples: (a) The number of blocked in dovecotes may vary. (b) Chimney detail depending on the amount of fettling involved (c) On the left side, the seated woman is sometimes headless. She lost all her detail towards the end of production and may have turned into a bush on some very late models. This is not a model of Wordworth's home in the Lake District — the name is coincidental.

SCULPTED: 1980
LOCATION: The Coalshed
RELEASED: 1980 RETIRED: 1983
SIZE: Width: 6 ¼" Depth: 5 ⅝" Height: 3 ½"
MARKINGS: None/ DOVE COTTAGE
© DAVID WINTER
ISSUE PRICE: £8 $60

DOWER HOUSE

In his book *Collecting David Winter Cottages*, John Hine grouped six Cottages together as a sub-collection and called them 'The Landowners' — Castle Gate, The Dower House, Falstaff's Manor, The Grange and Tudor Manor House. Gradually each piece retired and The Dower House was the last to go in May 1993. No variations or modifications are known to have been made during production.

SCULPTED: 1982
LOCATION: Hendon Road
RELEASED: 1982 RETIRED: May 1993
SIZE: Width: 3 ¼" Depth: 2" Height: 2 ½"
MARKINGS: © DAVID WINTER 1982
ISSUE PRICE: £6 $22

FAIRYTALE CASTLE

Numerous variations of this piece exist. Characteristics of early pieces: a) A foliage arch behind the main tower. b) Lack of foliage, especially between the towers. c) Sharply pointed towers. Then a series of modifications were made gradually over a three year period: a) The foliage arch was filled in and two others added during 1984/5. b) Foliage added, notably between the towers to prevent them from separating in the mould. c) Sharp tower points rounded off. The overall size diminished on pieces made between 1983 and '85 as mould shrinkage increased. The problem was then corrected and later pieces returned to the original size.

SCULPTED: 1982
LOCATION: Hendon Road
RELEASED: 1982 RETIRED: July 1989
SIZE: Width: 6" Depth: 5 ⅝" Height: 10"
MARKINGS: © DAVID WINTER 1982
ISSUE PRICE: £40 $115

FALSTAFF'S MANOR

A limited edition of 10,000 was announced in North America but not worldwide; numbered pieces were only sold in Canada and the USA. Production of all pieces ceased when the numbered allocation had been fulfilled in late 1990. The retirement was not declared, however, until unnumbered stock had depleted in early 1991. David started sculpting Falstaff's Manor in late 1985 (at the same time as he was remodelling Tudor Manor House) but didn't complete the work until the New Year, hence the base marking. It's one of his all-time favourite pieces and one of only a few he has on display in his own home. Watch out for spelling variations on the backstamp — Fallstaff's Manor and Falstaff Manor. There may be others.

SCULPTED: 1985/86
LOCATION: 19 Ash Street
RELEASED: 1986 RETIRED: 1990/91
SIZE: Width: 7" Depth: 6 ½" Height: 7 ¾"
MARKINGS: © DAVID WINTER 1986
ISSUE PRICE: £115 $242

THE FORGE

Variations: a) Later pieces have more foliage growing between the outhouse and the main thatched building. b) Clarity of the inscription on the milestone (BATH 104) on the front wall varies from early to late pieces due to mould deterioration; so too does the inscription on the sign (A SHILLING A SHOE) c) Early pieces had a name plaque with the inscription *THE FORGE © DAVID WINTER* (very rare).

SCULPTED: 1980
LOCATION: The Coalshed
RELEASED: 1980 RETIRED: 1983
SIZE: Width: 9" Depth: 5" Height: 2 ⅞"
MARKINGS: None
ISSUE PRICE: £9 $60

THE GRANGE

SCULPTED: 1988
LOCATION: Home Studio
RELEASED: 1988 RETIRED: June 1989
SIZE: Width: 5 ¼" Depth: 4" Height: 6 ⅝"
MARKINGS: © DAVID WINTER JULY 1988
ISSUE PRICE: £60 $120

The Grange was a production nightmare. Even before the launch in the summer of 1988 there were difficulties getting the complex metal balcony attachment to fit accurately onto the Crystacal, the problem being that Crystacal 'gives' and metal doesn't — each balcony had to be customised by John Hine's finishing department. Deliveries to shops were delayed, customers did not receive their orders, and everyone got hot under the collar. To discourage further orders, John Hine decided to double the price of the piece from £60 ($120) to £120 ($240). To his dismay, this had the very opposite effect and orders increased. His final card was to order a sudden death retirement, which took place on 20th June 1989. Pieces at the workshops were pulled from production and destroyed by John Hine in person, with help from his son Harry and Sales Director David Gravelle. (In a little over two days they smashed 1,000 completed pieces, and even more unpainted white stock). This created a frenzy amongst David Winter collectors never equalled before or since, with prices mushrooming overnight and eventually peaking at $4,500. Everyone seemed desperate to get the piece and T-shirts appeared stating *I'd give the shirt off my back for a Grange*. Prices have reached a more realistic level now, but it still remains a much sought-after piece, and in David Winter collecting circles, The Grange retains something of a mythical status.

THE HAYBARN

SCULPTED: 1983
LOCATION: Hendon Road
RELEASED: 1983 RETIRED: 1987
SIZE: Width: 4 ¼" Depth: 2 ½" Height: 3"
MARKINGS: DAVID WINTER
ISSUE PRICE: £6 $22

The inspiration for The Haybarn came from an illustration David saw in a book of a real barn dating back to the 1970s which had been preserved at the Welsh Folk Museum at St Fagan's, Cardiff. The same book also inspired Miner's Cottage.

HERMITS HUMBLE HOME

During the first year of production alterations were made to the trees. On later models gaps were filled in with greenery to make casting and demoulding easier. Hermits Humble Home, together with House of the Master Mason, House on Top and Woodcutter's Cottage are sometimes referred to by collectors as David's Fantasy Series — all very popular pieces on the secondary market. They were all retired on the same day — 1st June 1988.

SCULPTED: 1985
LOCATION: Hendon Road
RELEASED: 1985 RETIRED: June 1988
SIZE: Width: 4 ¹/₂" Depth: 3 ³/₄" Height: 5 ¹/₂"
MARKINGS: © DAVID WINTER 1985
ISSUE PRICE: £32 $87

HERTFORD COURT

. . . or 'Eric', as this piece is better known at John Hine Studios — a working title during pre-production that stuck. *Mould 1* Rare early models have a narrower courtyard, smaller centre section of the main building and less foliage generally. *Mould 2* The courtyard was widened to prevent the balcony from being pulled off during demoulding.

SCULPTED: 1983
LOCATION: Home Studio
RELEASED: 1983 RETIRED: August 1992
SIZE: Width: 5 ¹/₂" Depth: 3 ³/₄" Height: 5 ³/₄"
MARKINGS: © DAVID WINTER 1983
ISSUE PRICE: £30 $80

SCULPTED: 1984
LOCATION: Hendon Road
RELEASED: 1984 RETIRED: 1988
SIZE: Width: 5" Depth: 3 ³/₄" Height: 6 ¹/₂"
MARKINGS: © DAVID WINTER 1984
ISSUE PRICE: £32 $75

HOUSE OF THE MASTER MASON

Another of the so-called Fantasy Series. The pantiles, rendered walls and ostentatious chimney give this piece the sophistication you would expect from the home built for himself by a master mason.

HOUSE ON TOP

Also a so-called 'Fantasy' piece (see House of the Master Mason, Hermit's Humble Home and Woodcutter's Cottage). Rare early pieces have a sheer drop leading from just outside the double doors of the 'house on top' down into the cave below which was blocked up very soon into production. During the first two years, the gaps which originally existed behind the curved beams supporting the overhanging buildings were gradually filled in with greenery. By 1984 they had all been blocked up. Beyond the main double doors is a tunnel which leads right through to the other side of the piece, and halfway along the passage is a half door. This may be missing on later pieces as moulds were deteriorating towards the end of production. When this piece was sculpted in 1982 another company had just started producing miniature cottages and the name 'House On Top' is a veiled reference to the superiority of David Winter Cottages.

SCULPTED: 1982
LOCATION: Hendon Road
RELEASED: 1982 RETIRED: 1988
SIZE: Width: 4 $\frac{7}{8}$" Depth: 4 $\frac{1}{2}$" Height: 6 $\frac{1}{8}$"
MARKINGS: © DAVID WINTER 1982
ISSUE PRICE: £32 $92

SCULPTED: 1982
LOCATION: 19 Ash Street
RELEASED: 1982 RETIRED: October 1992
SIZE: Width: 3 $\frac{1}{2}$" Depth: 2 $\frac{1}{2}$" Height: 3 $\frac{1}{2}$"
MARKINGS: DAVID WINTER /
© DAVID WINTER 1982
ISSUE PRICE: £6 $20

IVY COTTAGE

Very early models are marginally taller than the main production run. The white stepping stones, window boxes, and the date on the base were not added until 1983. At the same time more of the ivy which gives the piece its name was added. By 1984 it had spread onto the roof, but this was removed on later models.

JOHN BENBOW'S FARM HOUSE

SCULPTED: 1987
LOCATION: Home Studio
RELEASED: 1987 RETIRED: August 1993
SIZE: Width: 5" Depth: 4 3/8" Height: 3 3/4"
MARKINGS: © DAVID WINTER 1987
ISSUE PRICE: £25 $55

Sculpted to commemorate the 150th anniversary of the British Mission of the Church of Latter-day Saints and dedicated to the memory of John Benbow, a Shropshire farmer who left England to join the Mormon community in Salt Lake City. 'Raffles', the David Winter stockist in Windsor, Berkshire, requested the piece following suggestions from their numerous Mormon customers. The piece was initially intended to be available only for one year exclusively from 'Raffles', but there was clearly a demand from other collectors and so it was added to the main collection. Pieces sold by 'Raffles' during the first year had a customised backstamp which was altered when 'Benbow's' went on general release. Excluding the Green Dragon pub sign, this is the first David Winter Cottage with a metal accessory; the timber supports to the porch.

SCULPTED: 1980
LOCATION: The Coalshed
RELEASED: 1980 RETIRED: 1983
SIZE: Width: 5 1/2" Depth: 3 3/4" Height: 2 1/2"
MARKINGS: None
ISSUE PRICE: £5 $27

LITTLE FORGE

This is a rare and sought-after piece and examples rarely appear on the secondary market. To sculpt Little Forge, David took The Forge and cut away everything apart from the main building — the wall, hedge, tree and stable all disappeared. He used this technique of cloning one piece from another several times during the first year or so, as the demand for a range of miniature cottages increased beyond David and John's wildest expectations; Mill House spawned Little Mill, from Market Street came Little Market and The Winemerchant, and The Coaching Inn was parent to Rose Cottage and Tudor Manor House.

LITTLE MARKET

SCULPTED: 1980
LOCATION: The Coalshed
(remodelled at Hendon Road)
RELEASED: 1980 REMODELLED: 1983
RETIRED: June 1993
SIZE: Width: 3 ¼" Depth: 3 ⅛" Height: 3"
MARKINGS: None / DAVID WINTER / © DAVID
WINTER 1980 / © DAVID WINTER 1983
ISSUE PRICE: £9 $27

Mould 1 David took a wax cast of Market Street, cut it in half and sculpted new detail where the two had joined together; the left became The Winemerchant and the right Little Market. Thus one David Winter Cottage became three in a short space of time. *Mould 2* In 1983 David remodelled the piece to restore some detail lost in aging moulds and to improve other detailing; beams were highlighted more, the chimney raised and enlarged and the piece made generally crisper.

LITTLE MILL
(Mould 1 - original)

The original Little Mill derived from the original Mill House. David cut away all the surrounding elements to leave just the T-shaped main building; even the water wheel disappeared. The piece has no markings and was superseded within months by two very different models with the same name. This original Little Mill is highly collectable.

SCULPTED: 1980
LOCATION: The Coalshed
RELEASED: 1980 RETIRED: 1980
SIZE: Width: 5 ¼" Depth: 4 ½" Height: 2 ¾"
MARKINGS: None
ISSUE PRICE: £5 $N/A

LITTLE MILL
(Moulds 2 & 3)

SCULPTED: 1980
LOCATION: The Coalshed
RELEASED: 1980 RETIRED: 1983
SIZE: Width: 5 ⅝" Depth: 3 ⅛" Height: 3"
MARKINGS: None
ISSUE PRICE: £5 $40

Little Mill Moulds 2 & 3 look very similar to each other but are so different from the original that it is right to classify them apart. The reason for this is that the original Little Mill derived from the original Mill House, whereas Moulds 2 & 3 derived from the much different remodelled version. Moulds 2 & 3 are rectangular in shape, the stem of the T having been removed. More importantly the water wheel has been replaced and they look far more like a mill. *Mould 2* has a name plaque at the rear of the base which reads *THE LITTLE MILL. DAVID WINTER 1980* . *Mould 3* has no name plaque. But the feature that distinguishes it clearly from Mould 2 is the addition of foliage between the water wheel and the mill building. This was done to simplify demoulding, the join on Mould 2 being delicate and easily broken. Mould 2 is the rarer and more collectable of the two, as secondary market prices reflect. See photograph overleaf. ➤

Retired Pieces

Little Mill (Mould 2)   Little Mill (Mould 3)

(See previous page)

MILL HOUSE
(Mould 1 - original)

The first Cottage ever sculpted by David Winter, in early 1980, and produced for a few months only. The bold plaque at the front reads *THE MILL HOUSE ENGLAND © DAVID WINTER* . It has none of the fine detail of later pieces and the smooth texture (beams flush with the walls, conical trees) suggest that David is thinking in terms of ceramics rather than the possibilities of Crystacal and silicon moulds. The original Mill House looks precisely what it is — a proto-type of things to come. Historically it has great significance, and rarity to match. Within months David had remodelled the piece and the original with its extensive base, river and outbuilding was produced in a very small quantity.

SCULPTED: 1980
LOCATION: The Coalshed
RELEASED: 1980 RETIRED: 1980
SIZE: Width: 9 ¼" Depth: 6 ½" Height: 3 ½"
MARKINGS: None
ISSUE PRICE: £7 $N/A

MILL HOUSE
(Mould 2)

Sculpted within a matter of months of the original, the remodelled Mill House shows how rapidly David's technique was developing at the time. The detailing is finer and more prominent, with beams raised away from wall level, a more complex water wheel and more realistic greenery. He has also pared away most of the base, losing the outhouse, river and surrounding land, suggesting that his future interest lies in buildings rather than rustic scenes. The remodelled Mill House is more commonly available on the secondary market than the original, having been in production for almost three years.

SCULPTED: 1980
LOCATION: The Coalshed
RELEASED: 1983 RETIRED: 1983
SIZE: Width: 8" Depth: 4 ⅝" Height: 3 ¼"
MARKINGS: © DAVID WINTER 1983
ISSUE PRICE: £8 $50

MINER'S COTTAGE

SCULPTED: 1982
LOCATION: Hendon Road
RELEASED: 1982 RETIRED: 1987
SIZE: Width: 3 $^3/_8$" Depth: 1 $^3/_8$" Height: 2 $^3/_8$"
MARKINGS: DAVID WINTER
ISSUE PRICE: £6 $22

Inspired by an illustration in a book which David borrowed from John Hine. The same book prompted David to sculpt The Haybarn.

THE OLD CURIOSITY SHOP

A model of the real Old Curiosity Curiosity Shop in Portsmouth Street, Lincoln's Inn, London, the building which inspired Charles Dickens to write his novel of the same name. In the early '80s David's piece could be purchased inside the shop itself. Nowadays it backs onto a modern office block and rather than fabricate the rear wall, David left it cut away to reveal the cluttered interior of the shop. On most models a man can be seen peering out from behind some curtains, but he is missing on a few early pieces. David sculpted a beautifully detailed window display behind the shop front which includes a model of his model of The Old Curiosity Shop. Numerous methods were tried to create a glass effect in the windows which would allow the display to be seen, resulting in five variations to the piece (in chronological order): *Mould 1* The window frame was cast as a separate piece and glued into place. Clear liquid imbedding resin was then poured through the windows and left to set hard. *Mould 2* Instead of pouring liquid resin through the windows, a thin sheet of hardened clear imbedding resin was sandwiched between the display and the glued-on window frame. *Mould 3*

MOORLAND COTTAGE

SCULPTED: 1982
LOCATION: Hendon Road
RELEASED: 1982
RETIRED: 1987
SIZE: Width: 2 $^3/_4$" Depth: 2 $^3/_4$"
Height: 2 $^1/_4$"
MARKINGS: DAVID WINTER
ISSUE PRICE: £6 $22

SCULPTED: 1980
LOCATION: David's parents' house
RELEASED: 1981 RETIRED: 1983
SIZE: Width: 4 $^3/_4$" Depth: 2 $^7/_8$" Height: 3 $^3/_4$"
MARKINGS: © DAVID WINTER 1980
ISSUE PRICE: £10 $40

Same as *2* but using a sheet of clear acetate instead of resin. *Mould 4* Same as *2* again but using clear bicycle reflector plastic instead of acetate. *Mould 5* All attempts to show the display were abandoned, it was filled in with Crystacal, the window frame attached permanently and the whole the piece cast as one.

THE OLD DISTILLERY

SCULPTED: 1982
LOCATION: Hendon Road
RELEASED: 1982 (RERELEASED 1989)
REMODELLED: 1986 RETIRED: February 1993
SIZE: Width: 10 ¼" Depth: 7 ½" Height: 9 ¼"
MARKINGS: © DAVID WINTER 1982
ISSUE PRICE: £95 $270

Mould 1 This piece was sculpted in 1982 but relaunched in 1989 to become part of the Scottish Collection. No alterations were made to the piece at that time apart from a restyled backstamp. (The word 'old' may also have been dropped from some backstamps.) Mould 2 Significant remodelling did take place, however, in 1986 when the following alterations were made: a) The most forward section of the building complex in the centre of the piece (between the two chimneys) was cut back by about half-an-inch and some crates added in the space. This was to prevent demoulding problems. b) On the left side, the back of the roof of the largest building was tapered, for the same reason. c) On the right side, more foliage was added in the centre of the group of buildings.

ONLY A SPAN APART

SCULPTED: 1990/91
LOCATION: Home Studio/Ireland
RELEASED: 1991 RETIRED: July 1993
SIZE: Width: 5 ³⁄₈" Depth: 3 ⁷⁄₈" Height: 4"
MARKINGS: © DAVID WINTER 1991
ISSUE PRICE: £38 $80

Under the working title 'Bridge to Peace', this model almost became special Guild Piece No. 9 when David's first attempt to create an Irish Collection was suspended in 1990. But it was replaced by Tomfool's Cottage and put on ice to become part of the Irish Collection launched in 1992, renamed Only A Span Apart. The piece was retired on the same day as Secret Shebeen, also from the Irish Collection.

ORCHARD COTTAGE

SCULPTED: 1986
LOCATION: North Studio, Eggars Hill
RELEASED: 1986 RETIRED: November 1991
SIZE: Width: 7 1/8" Depth: 4 3/4" Height: 4 3/4"
MARKINGS: © DAVID WINTER 1987
ISSUE PRICE: £42 $91

The only piece David has sculpted at Eggars Hill. He worked on it whilst the master mouldmaking department was in residence in the North Studio, but David cannot remember why he happened to be working there too!

SCULPTED: 1983
LOCATION: David's parents' home.
RELEASED: 1983 RETIRED: February 1993
SIZE: Width: 4" Depth: 4" Height: 4 1/8"
MARKINGS: © DAVID WINTER 1983
ISSUE PRICE: £12 $40

PILGRIM'S REST

David sculpted this piece in his parents' home, whilst his own home studio was being set up. This means that Pilgrim's Rest, a resting place for pilgrims making their way from Winchester to Canterbury to visit the tomb of Thomas Becket, was actually sculpted on the path they would have taken. The Winter family all live on the ancient route called The Pilgrims Way.

Retired Pieces

PROVENCAL ONE

SCULPTED: 1980
LOCATION: The Coalshed
RELEASED: 1981 RETIRED: 1981
SIZE: Width: 5" Depth: 3 ¾" Height: 3"
MARKINGS: None
ISSUE PRICE: £8 SN/A

David experienced the architecture of Provencal in the South of France personally on a visit with John Hine and his wife Rosie. The Provencal pieces are a curious quartet which stand apart from the conventional collection. They were sculpted for and sold almost entirely in the South of France where John Hine's son Harry was then living. He was given the job not only of casting them in situ but also of selling them at a local market. His enthusiasm for the project must have waned fairly quickly, few were sold and his remaining stock was tipped into a hole in the ground. A small number were also sold in the UK. Provencal Two has something of a reputation as incredibly rare, due mainly to the fact that not even John Hine Studios possess one. But Provencal One is just as impossible to track down and its value should not be underrated. Although no date markings exist on either of the large Provencal pieces, promotional material of the time proves they were sculpted in 1980, though not released until the following year. A lucky person won a Provencal One at the CARNIVAL '93 promotion, Warwick, in October 1993, as a treasure hunt prize.

Photography courtesy of John Hine Studios

PROVENCAL TWO

SCULPTED: 1980
LOCATION: The Coalshed
RELEASED: 1981 RETIRED: 1981
SIZE: Width: 7" Depth: 3 ½" Height: 3"
MARKINGS: DESSIN No.2 © DAVID WINTER
ISSUE PRICE: £8 SN/A

In 1989 John Hine launched a quest for a Provencal Two, this being the only piece he himself does not have on display at Eggars Hill — the intention being not to acquire the piece but at least to photograph it for posterity. A plea was published in the Guild magazine which is distributed worldwide; markets around the St Tropez area in the South of France, where Harry Hine sold them originally, were scoured; an advertisement was even place in the St Tropez local newspaper — without any response. Eventually there was a response, from a lady who lived within a half-hour drive of Eggars Hill! John Hine and Provencal were reunited, albeit briefly, and the piece was photographed. At the rear is a plaque with the words: *DESSIN NO.2 © DAVID WINTER.*

Photography courtesy of John Hine Studios

QUAYSIDE

Quayside ought not to be as difficult to find as it is, having been in production for five years. Nevertheless they are hard to come by and fetch good prices. No alterations in production are known to have been made, but painting variations are considerable between the soft tones of early pieces and the bolder style that had become standard by the mid-eighties.

SCULPTED: 1980
LOCATION: The Coalshed
RELEASED: 1980 RETIRED: 1985
SIZE: Width: 6 ³/₈" Depth: 3 ³/₄" Height: 4 ¹/₂"
MARKINGS: © DAVID WINTER 1980
ISSUE PRICE: £9 $52

SCULPTED: 1982
LOCATION: Hendon Road
RELEASED: 1982 RETIRED: 1982
SIZE: Width: 2" Depth: 2" Height: 2 ³/₄"
MARKINGS: FOR SABRINA GRAVELLE
25/3/82 DAVID WINTER
ISSUE PRICE: £6 $N/A

SABRINA'S COTTAGE

One of John Hine's early recruits into the company was David Gravelle who became a dad for the first time on 25th March 1982. David Winter sculpted a small piece which he thought might amuse the new baby, a girl called Sabrina, whose name and birth date were inscribed on the side of the cottage. Although intended purely as a personal gift, Sabrina's Cottage did find its way onto John Hine order forms and a small number were sold to shops. But they were reluctant to stock a piece which looked so different from David's usual cottages; Jonno Suart remembers driving all the way to Manchester with some amongst his van load . . . and returning with exactly the same number. Nowadays, of course, they are like gold dust. Should you ever have the opportunity of seeing more than one, you may notice there are painting variations to the eyes. A small number were made — as few as 100, John Hine recalls.

ST PAUL'S CATHEDRAL

A model of Sir Christopher Wren's architectural masterpiece in the City of London, sculpted by David to commemorate the wedding of Prince Charles to Lady Diana Spencer, 29th July 1981. A special wrap-around sleeve was produced for the box and the piece was available in at least one painting variation. As moulds began to deteriorate and bow slightly, later models were subject to distortion and loss of fine detail.

SCULPTED: 1981
LOCATION: 19 Ash Street
RELEASED: 1981 RETIRED: 1982
SIZE: Width: 5 ⁵⁄₈" Depth: 3 ¹⁄₄" Height: 3 ¹⁄₂"
MARKINGS: None
ISSUE PRICE: £9 $N/A

SECRET SHEBEEN

Secret Shebeen and Only A Span Apart were retired together in July 1993, something of a surprise for pieces only two years old and part of a collection (Irish). Both could well be worth acquiring as a future investment. A shebeen is an illicit drinking establishment where the infamous and very strong drink 'poteen' is distilled and consumed behind closed doors.

SCULPTED: 1991
LOCATION: Home Studio/Ireland
RELEASED: 1991 RETIRED: July 1993
SIZE: Width: 5 ¹⁄₂" Depth: 4 ¹⁄₈" Height: 4 ¹⁄₄"
MARKINGS: © DAVID WINTER 1991
ISSUE PRICE: £36 $70

SINGLE OAST

SCULPTED: 1981
LOCATION: 19 Ash Street
RELEASED: 1981 REMODELLED: (at Home Studio) 1985
RETIRED: October 1993
SIZE: Width: 4" Depth: 2 $^3/_4$" Height: 4 $^1/_2$"
MARKINGS: (original) DAVID WINTER /
(remodelled) © DAVID WINTER 1985
ISSUE PRICE: £7 $27

Mould 1 The original Single Oast had just David's signature on the base but no date, an open side door lying flat against the wall, no foliage and no white fence. *Mould 2* In 1985 a remodelled version was launched which included the date on the base, foliage, a fence and a side door standing slightly out from the wall. More significantly, the piece was restored to its original size; between 1981 and 1985 mould shrinkage had gradually reduced the piece by half-an-inch to the following dimensions: Width: 3 $^1/_2$" Depth: 2 $^1/_4$" Height: 4". A variety of materials have been used to make the wind vane — the same information applies to Triple Oast. On early models they are made of Crystacal, but this proved too fragile and few were made (examples are rarely found intact these days). A resin compound was used next, and then in 1986 they changed to metal. They are currently being made of plastic. The roof on early pieces was painted grey, but this was soon changed to the more common reddish brown.

SCULPTED: 1984
LOCATION: Hendon Road
RELEASED: 1984
RETIRED: September 1992
SIZE: Width: 5" Depth: 4 $^1/_4$" Height: 5 $^1/_2$"
MARKINGS: © DAVID WINTER 1984
ISSUE PRICE: £25 $65

SNOW COTTAGE

A few early pieces were sold with 'Christmas Cottage' on the backstamp. The name was changed to Snow Cottage in order that the piece might have an all-year-round appeal. The patches of tiles showing through the otherwise snow-covered roof are sometimes left unpainted by mistake, if a painter has failed to notice the desired effect. On some pieces the mouse may be missing from his precarious position on top of the chimney, due to wear and tear in production moulds.

SCULPTED: 1984
LOCATION: Home Studio
RELEASED: 1984 RETIRED: April 1991
SIZE: Width: 2 ½" Depth: 2 ⅛" Height: 4"
MARKINGS: © DAVID WINTER 1983
ISSUE PRICE: £9 $27

◄ SPINNER'S COTTAGE

Demoulders at John Hine Studios were not sad to see Spinner's Cottage retire. Although a seemingly innocuous little piece, the top is as wide as the base (possibly wider) and therefore difficult to extract without mishap.

SQUIRES HALL ➤

One of the 'Landowners', retired at the same time as Cotswold Village. Definitely not an acrophobic mouse on this piece!

SCULPTED: 1985
LOCATION: Home Studio
RELEASED: 1983 RETIRED: 1990
SIZE: Width: 5 ½" Depth: 4" Height: 6 ¾"
MARKINGS: © DAVID WINTER 1985
ISSUE PRICE: £37 $92

SUFFOLK HOUSE

SCULPTED: 1985
LOCATION: HENDON ROAD
RELEASED: 1985 RETIRED: JULY 1989
SIZE: WIDTH: 3 ⅝" DEPTH: 3" HEIGHT: 4 ¼"
MARKINGS: © DAVID WINTER 1985
ISSUE PRICE: £22 $49

At first the plaster walls were painted pale pink, then for a short while they changed to white. Finally they resorted to pink again but a darker shade than the original. 'Whites are slightly more valuable than 'pinks' on the secondary market. A pale orange variation also exists; its value is unknown, but as a true rarity must equate to that of a 'white' — or even higher.

THREE DUCKS INN

Three Ducks Inn is a prize for any ardent David Winter collector. Although there are no base marking on the piece, its name is to be seen clearly above the front entrance. The less defined the detail, the later the piece. Towards the end of production the wording on the two doors — SNUG and SALOON BAR — disappeared altogether. Only the third piece sculpted by David, Three Ducks Inn has some delightful touches, such as the post box sunk into the right-hand wall, and the seats and tables at the back made from barrels sawn in two.

SCULPTED: 1980
LOCATION: The Coalshed
RELEASED: 1980 RETIRED: 1983
SIZE: Width: 7 $\frac{3}{8}$" Depth: 5 $\frac{3}{8}$" Height: 3 $\frac{1}{4}$"
MARKINGS: None
ISSUE PRICE: £8 $N/A

TOLLKEEPER'S COTTAGE

During 1983 and 1984 more foliage was added to the piece generally. At one time a picture of Tollkeeper's Cottage accidentally printed in reverse in the Guild magazine caused suspicion amongst eagle-eyed collectors that the piece had been remodelled in some strange way.

SCULPTED: 1983
LOCATION: Hendon Road
RELEASED: 1984 RETIRED: May 1992
SIZE: Width: 5" Depth: 3 $\frac{7}{8}$" Height: 6"
MARKINGS: © DAVID WINTER 1983
ISSUE PRICE: £30 $75

TUDOR MANOR HOUSE

SCULPTED: 1981
LOCATION: David's parents' house (remodelled at 19 Ash Street)
RELEASED: 1981 REMODELLED: 1985
RETIRED: August 1992
SIZE: Width: 4 3/4" Depth: 3 1/2" Height: 4 1/2"
MARKINGS: © DAVID WINTER 1981
ISSUE PRICE: £6 $47

Mould 1 David sculpted Tudor Manor House on the dining room table at his parents' house, although the extensive remodelling took place at 19 Ash Street. The first few pieces cast (no more than a dozen, according to David) had tunnels passing through both side walls in line with the central balcony to form a walkway stretching the entire width of the piece. But this proved tricky to demould and the tunnels were blocked in (*Mould 2*). Pieces were originally cast with the balcony cast separately and glued into place, until mouldmaking had become sophisticated enough for the piece to be cast as a whole (*Mould 3*). At some unknown stage the piece lost the name plaque on the right rear corner. *Mould 4* Then in 1985 David completely remodelled the piece along these lines: (a) Foliage added (the original has none) (b) Chimney squared off and increased in height by half-an-inch (c) One of the two sets of stairs between the forked chimney breast removed (d) Bay window at front removed (e) Cellar window added front right (f) Staircases at front widened (g) All windows, three gables on inner roof and beamwork enlarged (h) Doorway under right balcony made smaller (j) Low brick walls at front extended (k) Some beams removed entirely.

TYTHE BARN

SCULPTED: 1981
LOCATION: 19 Ash Street
RELEASED: 1981 RETIRED: 1986
SIZE: Width: 6 1/4" Depth: 4" Height: 3 1/2"
MARKINGS: DAVID WINTER
ISSUE PRICE: £11 $39

A model of Park Farm Barn, Kingsley, just a few miles from the John Hine Studios sites in Bordon, Hampshire. The old barn was dilapidated in 1981 when David sculpted it and thirteen years on little has changed. Matchsticks were used for the posts supporting the covered area, but they were later cast in Crystacal and glued into place (similar to The Coaching Inn). The two horses' heads protruding from the stables on the right front of the piece were very difficult to demould intact and either one or both are commonly missing. (They are actually toy dogs which David incorporated into his original wax sculpture.) Two versions of Tythe Barn exist usually referred to as 'Door On' and 'Door Off', a reference to the right-hand side of the main double doors. *Mould 1* DOOR ON. David sculpted the right side door standing ajar, but this was also difficult

to cast and demould intact, with the door frequently snapping off. Consequently production was sluggish. Collectors also found (still do!) that the slightest touch is enough to bring disaster. Before the piece was modified to solve the problem, an intermediary stage was tried for a while with the door cast separately and glued into place. The door varies in position from almost shut to wide open. *Mould 2* DOOR OFF. In 1983 it was decided to remove the door and David sculpted it lying on the ground, as if it had been blown off its hinges. 'Door Off's are more commonly found than 'Door On's and this is reflected in the value. Tythe Barn has always been in demand with collectors and its retirement in 1986 can be seen as the starting point for serious interest in the David Winter Cottages secondary market.

Retired Pieces

Tythe Barn (Door On)

WILLIAM SHAKESPEARE'S BIRTHPLACE
(Large)

Having sculpted a Tiny version two years earlier, David produced a larger model of William Shakespeare's Birthplace, Stratford-Upon-Avon, one of England's most visited tourist attractions, in 1982. The David Winter Cottages stockist in Stratford had a distinct advantage in selling this piece as the shop was located immediately opposite the real building. In sculpting 'Shakespeare Large' (as it is sometimes called), David acknowledges the help of Tim Moore, the Master Mouldmaker at John Hine Studios for many years. Tim blocked up the piece and attached all the tiles, leaving David to add all the remaining detail. At about the same time, Tim was also responsible for sculpting in its entirety a large version of Anne Hathaway's Cottage which was marketed by John Hine Studios alongside the David Winter Cottages collection. The base is clearly marked with the initials T.M. (plus a symbol of inter-locking circles). John Hine Studios subsequently released a medium-sized William Shakespeare's Birthplace, which is sometimes thought to be a 'David Winter'; however, it is the work of Malcolm Cooper (he of Great British Pubs fame).

SCULPTED: 1982
LOCATION: 19 Ash Street
RELEASED: 1982 RETIRED: 1984
SIZE: Width: 6 ³/₈" Depth: 4 ⁷/₈" Height: 3 ¹/₄"
MARKINGS: © DAVID WINTER 1980
ISSUE PRICE: £20 $60

61

THE WINEMERCHANT

The name on the shop sign is Fred'k Venzer, a variation on David's father's name — Frederick Winter. *Mould 1* A few of the first pieces made have weatherboarding on the front, similar to the final remodelled version, but this was replaced by beamwork early into production (*Mould 2*). *Mould 3* During remodelling in 1983, the following changes were made: (a) Beams on front facade replaced by weatherboarding (b) Windows restyled (c) Chimneys enlarged and raised to protrude above roof level (d) Foliage added generally, especially at front right and along the back wall (e) Horizontal and diagonal cross bars on back door removed. The wording on the shop sign was also restyled at some stage, though not necessarily when the remodelling took place.

SCULPTED: 1983
LOCATION: Home Studio
RELEASED: 1983 RETIRED: 1988
SIZE: Width: 4 ¹/₂" Depth: 4 ¹/₄" Height: 5 ⁷/₈"
MARKINGS: © DAVID WINTER 1984
ISSUE PRICE: £33 $87

SCULPTED: 1980
LOCATION: The Coalshed
(remodelled at Hendon Road)
RELEASED: 1980 REMODELLED: 1983
RETIRED: March 1993
SIZE: Width: 3 ¹/₂" Depth: 2 ¹/₂" Height: 4 ¹/₈"
MARKINGS: None / © DAVID WINTER 1980
ISSUE PRICE: £9 $27

WOODCUTTERS COTTAGE

'Bert' was the working title for this piece; it was also known as 'Tree House' before the name Woodcutter's Cottage was eventually decided upon. One of the so-called Fantasy Series (together with House of the Master Mason, Hermit's Humble Home and House On Top. *Mould 1* Early pieces (1983 to '85) have a sharper point to the highest tree stump at centre. *Mould 2* The tip was rounded off to avoid demoulding problems.

TINY SERIES

An early range of small pieces which, apart from Provencal A and B, all represent existing buildings.

ANNE HATHAWAY'S COTTAGE

The first few models had a marginally taller chimney, but it was very soon shortened to stop them from breaking off during demoulding. Shakespeare's wife was born and brought up in this beautiful thatched cottage in the village of Shottery, just outside Stratford-Upon-Avon and about two miles from Shakespeare's Birthplace. (John Hine Studios also produced a large version of Anne Hathaway's Cottage, sculpted by Tim Moore.)

SCULPTED: 1980
LOCATION: The Coalshed
RELEASED: 1980 RETIRED: 1982
SIZE: Width: 3 ³/₈" Depth: 1 ³/₄" Height: 1 ³/₈"
MARKINGS: © D.W.
ISSUE PRICE: £2 $N/A

COTSWOLD FARMHOUSE

SCULPTED: 1980
LOCATION: The Coalshed
RELEASED: 1980
RETIRED: 1982
SIZE: Width: 1 ⁵/₈" Depth: 1 ³/₄" Height: 1 ³/₈"
MARKINGS: © D.W.
ISSUE PRICE: £2 $N/A

A real building somewhere in the Cotswolds — the precise where-abouts is lost in the mists of time. This was the first of the Tiny Series sculpted by David.

SCULPTED: 1980
LOCATION: The Coalshed
RELEASED: 1980 RETIRED: 1982
SIZE: Width: 2 ⁷/₈" Depth: 1 ³/₄" Height: 1 ³/₈"
MARKINGS: © D.W.
ISSUE PRICE: £2 $N/A

CROWN INN

Has the inscription *CROWN INN CHID-DINGFOLD AD 1285* sculpted into the base at the front. The village of Chiddingfold, where the real Crown Inn can be found, is on the Surrey/Sussex border, on the road between Godalming and Petworth. A nice place for lunch.

Retired Pieces

WILLIAM SHAKESPEARE'S BIRTHPLACE

SCULPTED: 1980
LOCATION: The Coalshed
RELEASED: 1980 RETIRED: 1982
SIZE: Width: 2 ⁵/₈" Depth: 1 ⁵/₈" Height: 1 ¹/₄"
MARKINGS: © D.W.
ISSUE PRICE: £2 $N/A

The first version by David of Shakespeare's Birthplace; a larger version was sculpted and released in 1982.

ST NICHOLAS' CHURCH

SCULPTED: 1980
LOCATION: The Coalshed
RELEASED: 1980 RETIRED: 1982
SIZE: Width: 3" Depth: 1 ³/₄" Height: 1 ³/₄"
MARKINGS: © D.W. ISSUE PRICE: £2 $N/A

A model of St Nicholas' Church in the Surrey village of Compton, near Godalming. As well as ordinary pieces, white stock (unpainted models) were sold as wedding cake decorations in Compton village shop, to appeal to couples who were getting married in the church. Colour variations exist: the wooden shingles around the steeple of the real church were sometimes painted as if they were tiles.

SULGRAVE MANOR

SCULPTED: 1980
LOCATION: The Coalshed
RELEASED: 1980 RETIRED: 1982
SIZE: Width: 3 ¹/₄" Depth: 2" Height: 1 ³/₈"
MARKINGS: © D.W. ISSUE PRICE: £2 $N/A

The Ancestral home of George Washington in Northamptonshire. The family coat of arms sculpted into the front of the base proved difficult and time consuming to paint, so John Hine test marketed an unpainted terracotta version with their Guildford stockist (David Windsor). It did not sell and barely a handful were made.

PROVENCAL A & PROVENCAL B

SCULPTED: 1981
LOCATION: The Coalshed
RELEASED: 1981 RETIRED: 1981
SIZE: A — Width: 2 ³/₄" Depth: 1 ¹/₂" Height: 1 ¹/₄"
B — Width: 2 ⁷/₈" Depth: 1 ¹/₄" Height: 1 ⁵/₈"
MARKINGS: © D.W. A / © D.W. B ISSUE PRICE: £3 $N/A

Two 'Tiny' pieces sculpted to complement the larger Provencal One and Provencal Two and available almost exclusively in the South of France. Provencal A and Provencal B were sculpted after and retired before the other six 'Tinies' — hence their higher value. All four Provencals are very rare.

Checklist

A complete reference list of all David Winter Cottages and associated items. Use the tick boxes to keep check of everything in your collection. Extremely rare items such as one-off pieces are not included. Cottages are listed alphabetically within year of release. Retired pieces are in italics.

NAME

1980

- *The Coaching Inn* ☐
- *Dove Cottage* ☐
- *The Forge* ☐
- *Little Forge* ☐
- *Little Market* ☐
- *Little Mill (Mould 1)* ☐
- *Little Mill (Mould 2/3)* ☐
- *Market Street* ☐
- *Mill House (Mould 1)* ☐
- *Mill House (Mould 2)* ☐
- *Quayside* ☐
- *Rose Cottage* ☐
- *Three Ducks Inn* ☐

- *TINY SERIES* ☐
- *Anne Hathaway's Cottage* ☐
- *The Crown Inn* ☐
- *Cotswold Farmhouse* ☐
- *St. Nicholas Church* ☐
- *Sulgrave Manor* ☐
- *William Shakespeare's Birthplace* ☐

- *The Winemerchant* ☐

1981

- *Castle Keep* ☐
- *Chichester Cross* ☐
- *Cornish Cottage* ☐
- *Double Oast* ☐
- *The Old Curiosity Shop* ☐
- *Provencal One* ☐
- *Provencal Two* ☐
- *Provencal A* ☐
- *Provencal B* ☐
- *St Paul's Cathedral* ☐
- Single Oast ☐
- Stratford House ☐

NAME

- Triple Oast ☐
- Tudor Manor House ☐
- Tythe Barn ☐
- The Village ☐

1982

- *Blacksmith's Cottage* ☐
- *Brookside Hamlet* ☐
- *Cotswold Cottage* ☐
- *Cotswold Village* ☐
- *The Dower House* ☐
- *Drover's Cottage* ☐
- *Fairytale Castle* ☐
- *House On Top* ☐
- *Ivy Cottage* ☐
- *The Old Distillery* ☐
- *Moorland Cottage* ☐
- *Sabrina's Cottage* ☐
- *Sussex Cottage* ☐
- *The Village Shop* ☐
- *W. Shakespeare's Birthplace (large)* ☐

1983

- *The Alms Houses* ☐
- The Bakehouse ☐
- The Bothy ☐
- *The Cotton Mill* ☐
- *Cornish Tin Mine* ☐
- Fisherman's Wharf ☐
- The Green Dragon Inn ☐
- *The Haybarn* ☐
- Hertford Court ☐
- *Miner's Cottage* ☐
- *Pilgrim's Rest* ☐

1984

- Castle Gate ☐

65

The Chapel ❏
House of the Master Mason ❏
The Parsonage ❏
Snow Cottage ❏
Spinner's Cottage ❏
Tollkeeper's Cottage ❏
Woodcutters Cottage ❏

1985
The Apothecary Shop ❏
Blackfriars Grange ❏
The Cooper's Cottage ❏
Craftsmen's Cottages ❏
Hermits Humble Home ❏
The Hogs Head Tavern ❏
Kent Cottage ❏
Meadowbank Cottages ❏
St George's Church ❏
The Schoolhouse ❏
Shirehall ❏
Squires Hall ❏
Suffolk House ❏
The Vicarage ❏
Yeoman's Farmhouse ❏

1986
Falstaff's Manor ❏
There was a Crooked House ❏
Village Scene - Point of Sale ❏

1987
Devon Combe ❏
Devon Creamery ❏
Ebenezer Scrooge's Counting House ❏
John Benbow's Farm House ❏
Orchard Cottage ❏
Smuggler's Creek ❏
Tamar Cottage ❏

1988
Bottle Kilns ❏
Christmas in Scotland and Hogmanay ❏
(Coal)miner's Row ❏
Cornish Engine House ❏
Cornish Harbour ❏
Crofters Cottage ❏
Derbyshire Cotton Mill ❏
The Grange ❏
Gunsmiths ❏
Lacemakers ❏

Lock-Keeper's Cottage ❏
The Windmill ❏
Wintershill (Jim'll Fix It) ❏

1989
A Christmas Carol ❏
Gatekeepers ❏
Gillie's Cottage ❏
The House on the Loch ❏
MacBeth's Castle ❏
Scottish Crofters ❏

1990
The Boat House ❏
Burns Reading Room ❏
Blossom Cottage ❏
The Bull and Bush ❏
Cartwright's Cottage ❏
Grouse Moor Lodge ❏
Guy Fawkes ❏
Harvest Barn ❏
Knight's Castle ❏
Mister Fezziwig's Emporium ❏
Pudding Cottage ❏
St Anne's Well ❏
Staffordshire Vicarage ❏
Stonecutters Cottage ❏

1991
Bookends ❏
CASTLE IN THE AIR ❏
Fred's Home ❏
Gatekeepers Colourway ❏
Inglenook Cottage ❏
Moonlight Haven ❏
The Weaver's Lodgings ❏

1992
Audrey's Tea Room ❏
Birthstone Wishing Well ❏
Cameos
Barley Malt Kiln ❏
Brooklet Bridge ❏
Greenwood Wagon ❏
Lych Gate ❏
Market Day ❏
One Man Jail ❏
The Potting Shed ❏
Poultry Ark ❏
The Privy ❏

NAME

Saddle Steps	☐
Welsh Pig Pen	☐
Fogartys	☐
Irish Round Tower	☐
Mad Baron Fourthrite's Folly	☐
Murphys	☐
O'Donovan's Castle	☐
Only A Span Apart	☐
Scrooge's School	☐
Secret Shebeen	☐

1993

Arches Thrice	☐
Birth Day Cottage	☐
The Castle Cottage of Warwick	☐
Horatio Pernickety's Amorous Intent	☐
Old Joe's Beetling Shop	☐
Plum Cottage	☐

Scenes

Christmas Scene	☐
At The Bakehouse	☐
At The Bothy	☐
At Rose Cottage	☐

The Shires

Berkshire Milking Byre	☐
Buckinghamshire Bull Pen	☐
Derbyshire Dovecote	☐
Cheshire Kennels	☐
Gloucestershire Greenhouse	☐
Hampshire Hutches	☐
Lancashire Donkey Shed	☐
Oxfordshire Goat Yard	☐
Shropshire Pig Shelter	☐
Staffordshire Stable	☐
Wiltshire Waterwheel	☐
Yorkshire Sheep Fold	☐

1994

The English Village	☐
The 'Cat and Pipe' Inn	☐
The Chandlery	☐
The Church and Vestry	☐
The Constabulary	☐
Crystal Cottage	☐
The Engine House	☐
Glebe Cottage	☐
The Hall	☐

NAME

One Acre Cottage	☐
The Post Office	☐
The Quack's Cottage	☐
The Rectory	☐
The Seminary	☐
The Smithy	☐
The Tannery	☐
Guardian Castle	☐
15th Anniversary Piece	☐

GUILD SPECIAL PIECES

1987	
Village Scene - Guild version	☐
Robin Hood's Hideaway	☐
Queen Elizabeth Slept Here	☐
1988	
Black Bess Inn	☐
The Pavilion	☐
1989	
Street Scene/Bas-Relief Plaque	☐
Home Guard	☐
The Coal Shed	☐
1990	
The Plucked Ducks	☐
The Cobbler	☐
The Pottery	☐
1991	
Pershore Mill	☐
Tomfool's Cottage	☐
Will-'o-the-wisp	☐
1992	
Irish Water Mill	☐
The Beekeeper's	☐
The Candlemaker's	☐
1993	
On the Riverbank	☐
Thameside	☐☐
Swan Upping Cottage	☐
1994	
15 Lawnside Road	☐
Whileaway Cottage	☐
Ashe Cottage	☐

OTHER ITEMS

Village Scene - Point of Sale	☐
Christmas Ornaments	
(not by David Winter)	
1991 Set	☐
1992 Set	☐

Checklist

1993 Set ❏

COMMONLY AVAILABLE MEMORABILIA
Audio Cassettes
The Mad Baron Spectacular ❏

Cottage Country magazines
1987
Spring (1) ❏
Summer (2) ❏
Autumn (3) ❏
Winter (4) ❏
1988
Spring (5) ❏
Summer (6) ❏
Autumn (7) ❏
Winter (8) ❏
1989
Spring (9) ❏
Summer (10) ❏
Autumn (11) ❏
Winter (12) ❏
1990
Spring (13) ❏
Summer (14) ❏
Autumn (15) ❏
Winter (16) ❏
1991
Spring (17) ❏
Summer (18) ❏
Autumn (19) ❏
Winter (20) ❏
1992
Spring (21) ❏
Summer (22) ❏
Autumn (23) ❏
Winter (24) ❏
1993
Spring (25) ❏
Summer (26) ❏
Autumn (27) ❏
Winter (28) ❏
1994
Spring (29) ❏
Summer (30) ❏
Autumn (31) ❏
Winter (32) ❏

The Directory ❏
Mouse Pin ❏

The Plate Collection
Chichester Cross ❏
A Christmas Carol ❏
Cotswold Village ❏
Dove Cottage ❏
Ebenezer Scrooge's Counting House ❏
The Forge ❏
Little Mill ❏
The Old Curiosity Shop ❏

Retired Range Binder ❏

Toby Jugs
David Winter ❏
The Pershore Miller ❏
Videos
Mad Baron Spectacular ❏
Meet the Artist ❏

BOOKS
The Collectors Book/Catalogue (1985) ❏
Collecting David Winter Cottages
(1989) - John Hine ❏
Collectors Pocket Book (1989) ❏
The Tale of Pershore Mill (1991) -
John Hine ❏
The David Winter Cottages Handbook
(1992) - John Hughes ❏
Baroness Hardunbuy's Book of Happy
Times Ahead (1992) - John Hine ❏
Mad Baron Fourthrite's Family History
(1992) - John Hine ❏
Inside David Winter Cottages (1993) -
John Hughes ❏

RARE MEMORABILIA
Audio Cassettes
Burns Poetry ❏
The Maids of Pershore Mill ❏

Collectors' Catalogue Cards ❏
Card Dispenser ❏
David Winter (Seaside) Rock ❏
Guild Pipe & Smoking Kit ❏
Guild Sweat Shirts ❏
Table Mats & Coasters ❏
Village Memories (magazine) ❏

Issue Prices of Current Pieces

Listed here are the first issue prices of all current David Winter Cottages and the recommended selling prices established by John Hine Studios for 1994. Prices that include pence/cents have been rounded up to the nearest pound/dollar. Pieces marked with an asterisk (*) were not widely available outside the UK before 1984. In these cases, the first issue price quoted in US dollars dates from 1984/85 and not the year of issue.

The earliest recommended/suggested selling prices available for consultation were 1988 in the USA and 1986 in the UK. All issue prices prior to these dates have been recon-structed from 'factory gate' prices (or rather 'workshop gate' prices).

There are some interesting comparisons to be made. In the UK, for example, Rose Cottage has increased in value sixfold from £5 to £30, whilst The Village has trebled from £95 to £300. Those original issue prices seem tantalisingly low today, but whether or not they are relatively cheaper in real terms is a matter for conjecture. In the space of a decade (1984-1994) the same two pieces have almost doubled in the United States (Rose Cottage — $30 to $52: The Village — $300 to $578).

NAME	YEAR OF ISSUE	FIRST ISSUE PRICE		1994 PRICES	
		UK £	US $	UK £	US $
ROSE COTTAGE	'80*	5	30	28	52
MARKET STREET	'80*	8	45	40	84
TRIPLE OAST	'81*	120	45	58	112
STRATFORD HOUSE	'81*	200	55	55	124
THE VILLAGE	'81*	95	300	300	578
DROVER'S COTTAGE	'82*	5	25	13	32
SUSSEX COTTAGE	'82*	6	25	19	40
THE VILLAGE SHOP	'82*	5	25	13	32
COTSWOLD COTTAGE	'82*	5	25	32	13
THE BAKEHOUSE	'83*	9	35	30	56
THE BOTHY	'83*	9	35	30	56
FISHERMAN'S WHARF	'83*	9	35	30	56

NAME	YEAR OF ISSUE	FIRST ISSUE PRICE		1994 PRICES	
		UK £	US $	UK £	US $
THE GREEN DRAGON INN	'83*	9	35	30	56
THE PARSONAGE	'94	120	350	270	556
KENT COTTAGE	'85	22	60	48	98
THERE WAS A CROOKED HOUSE	'86	40	140	70	152
MOONLIGHT HAVEN	'91	50	120	60	138
CASTLE IN THE AIR	'91	350	675	360	708
INGLENOOK COTTAGE	'91	30	60	33	70
THE WEAVER'S LODGINGS	'91	33	65	33	76
HEART OF ENGLAND SERIES					
THE SCHOOLHOUSE	'85	10	24	22	44
CRAFTSMEN'S COTTAGES	'85	10	24	19	40
THE VICARAGE	'85	10	24	19	40
THE HOGS HEAD TAVERN	'85	10	24	22	44
BLACKFRIARS GRANGE	'85	10	24	19	40
SHIREHALL	'85	10	24	22	44
THE APOTHECARY SHOP	'85	10	24	22	44
YEOMAN'S FARMHOUSE	'85	10	24	19	40
MEADOWBANK COTTAGES	'85	10	24	19	40
ST. GEORGE'S CHURCH	'85	10	24	22	44
THE WINDMILL	'88	14	38	28	52
WEST COUNTRY COLLECTION					
SMUGGLERS CREEK	'87	145	390	250	514
DEVON COMBE	'87	30	73	50	112

NAME	YEAR OF ISSUE	FIRST ISSUE PRICE		1994 PRICES	
		UK £	US $	UK £	US $
TAMAR COTTAGE	'87	16	45	33	74
DEVON CREAMERY	'87	25	63	48	98
CORNISH ENGINE HOUSE	'88	46	120	70	152
CORNISH HARBOUR	'88	46	120	70	152
MIDLANDS COLLECTION					
LOCK-KEEPER'S COTTAGE	'88	24	58	40	84
DERBYSHIRE COTTON MILL	'88	24	58	40	84
GUNSMITHS	'88	28	71	45	98
LACEMAKERS	'88	46	108	70	152
(COAL) MINERS ROW	'88	34	82	50	112
SCOTTISH COLLECTION					
THE HOUSE ON THE LOCH	'89	22	65	40	84
MACBETH'S CASTLE	'89	78	200	115	256
GILLIES COTTAGE	'89	24	65	40	84
GATEKEEPERS	'89	24	65	40	84
SCOTTISH CROFTERS	'89	19	42	30	56
BRITISH TRADITIONS					
BURNS' READING ROOM	'90	16	31	19	36
STONECUTTER'S COTTAGE	'90	24	48	30	54
THE BOAT HOUSE	'90	21	38	30	44
PUDDING COTTAGE	'90	43	78	45	90
BLOSSOM COTTAGE	'90	30	59	30	68
KNIGHT'S CASTLE	'90	30	59	38	68

NAME	YEAR OF ISSUE	FIRST ISSUE PRICE		1994 PRICES	
		UK £	US $	UK £	US $
ST ANNE'S WELL	'90	24	48	30	54
GROUSE MOOR LODGE	'90	24	48	30	54
STAFFORDSHIRE VICARAGE	'90	24	48	30	54
HARVEST BARN	'90	16	31	19	36
GUY FAWKES	'90	16	31	19	36
THE BULL AND BUSH	'90	18	38	20	44
CAMEOS					
LYCH GATE	'92	6	13	7	14
THE PRIVY	'92	6	13	7	14
THE POTTING SHED	'92	6	13	7	14
ONE MAN JAIL	'92	6	13	7	14
BARLEY MALT KILN	'92	6	13	7	14
POULTRY ARK	'92	6	13	7	14
WELSH PIG PEN	'92	6	13	7	14
MARKET DAY	'92	6	13	7	14
BROOKLET BRIDGE	'92	6	13	7	14
GREENWOOD WAGON	'92	6	13	7	14
SADDLE STEPS	'92	6	13	7	14
PENNY WISHING WELL	'92	6	13	7	14
DIORAMA	'92	25	52	28	54
IRISH COLLECTION					
IRISH ROUND TOWER	'92	30	65	33	68
FOGARTYS	'92	36	75	40	78

NAME	YEAR OF ISSUE	FIRST ISSUE PRICE		1994 PRICES	
		UK £	US $	UK £	US $
MURPHYS	'92	45	100	45	106
O'DONOVAN'S CASTLE	'92	73	145	82	152
THE SHIRES					
SHROPSHIRE PIG SHELTER	'93	15	32	20	32
OXFORDSHIRE GOAT YARD	'93	18	32	20	32
HAMPSHIRE HUTCHES	'93	18	34	20	34
WILTSHIRE WATERWHEEL	'93	18	34	20	34
CHESHIRE KENNELS	'93	18	36	20	36
DERBYSHIRE DOVECOTE	'93	18	36	20	36
STAFFORDSHIRE STABLE	'93	18	36	20	36
BERKSHIRE MILKING BYRE	'93	20	38	20	38
BUCKINGHAMSHIRE BULL PEN	'93	20	38	20	38
YORKSHIRE SHEEP FOLD	'93	20	38	20	38
LANCASHIRE DONKEY SHED	'93	20	38	20	38
GLOUCESTERSHIRE GREENHOUSE	'93	20	40	20	40
DAVID WINTER SCENES					
AT THE BOTHY - Vignette Base	'93	20	39	20	39
Farmer and Plough		44	60	44	60
Farm Hand and Spade		30	40	44	40
Farmer's Wife		33	45	33	45
Goose Girl		33	45	33	45
AT THE BAKEHOUSE Vignette Base	'93	18	35	18	35
Hot Cross Bun Seller		44	60	44	60

NAME	YEAR OF ISSUE	FIRST ISSUE PRICE		1994 PRICES	
		UK £	US $	UK £	US $
Woman at Pump		33	45	33	45
Lady Customer		33	45	33	45
Small Boy and Dog		33	45	33	45
Girl Selling Eggs		22	30	22	30
AT ROSE COTTAGE - Vignette Base	'93	20	39	20	39
Mother		39	50	37	50
Father		33	45	33	45
Son		22	30	22	30
Daughter		22	30	22	30
CHRISTMAS SCENE - Vignette Base	'93	20	50	20	50
Miss Belle		25	35	25	35
Bob Cratchit and Tiny Tim		35	50	35	50
Fred		25	35	25	35
Mrs Fezziwig		25	35	25	35
Tom the Street Shoveller		40	60	40	60
Ebenezer Scrooge		30	45	30	45
WELSH COLLECTION					
Y DDRAIG GOCH	'93	44	88	45	88
PEN-Y-GRAIG	'93	44	88	45	88
TYDDYN SYRIOL	'93	44	88	45	88
A BIT OF NONSENSE	'93	25	52	26	52
THE ENGLISH VILLAGE					
THE SMITHY	'93	30	50	28	50

NAME	YEAR OF ISSUE	FIRST ISSUE PRICE		1994 PRICES	
		UK £	US $	UK £	US $
THE TANNERY	'93	30	50	28	50
THE HALL	'93	35	55	30	55
ONE ACRE COTTAGE	'93	35	55	30	55
THE RECTORY	'93	35	55	30	55
THE CHURCH AND VESTRY	'94	30	57	30	57
GLEBE COTTAGE	'94	28	53	28	53
THE QUACK'S COTTAGE	'94	30	57	30	57
THE 'CAT AND PIPE' INN	'94	28	53	28	53
THE CONSTABULARY	'94	30	60	30	60
THE SEMINARY	'94	30	57	30	57
THE CHANDLERY	'94	28	53	28	53
CRYSTAL COTTAGE	'94	28	53	28	53
THE POST OFFICE	'94	28	53	28	53
THE ENGINE HOUSE	'93	28	55	28	55
GUARDIAN CASTLE					
15th ANNIVERSARY PIECE					

NAME	YEAR OF ISSUE	FIRST ISSUE PRICE		1994 PRICES	
		UK £	US $	UK £	US $

Current Pieces

This section lists all pieces sculpted by David Winter which are still commercially available in stores in Spring 1994. The term Mould 1, 2, 3 etc. is used to determine variations of a piece when they involve a specific modification, but not if changes were made gradually over a period of time. In these cases it is the most recent Mould that is still available. The first twenty pieces listed are not associated with specific collections and are listed chronologically.

ROSE COTTAGE

Mould 1 The original version had a name plaque ("ROSE COTTAGE") on the left front corner, a squatter chimney, a plant on the side wall and a window between the two levels of thatch. *Mould 2* Remodelling was necessary due to loss of detail in the moulds; the chimney was raised, and the plaque, plant and side window removed. For a long time the circular white paving stones were listed as having been added during remodelling, but they are in fact to be see on the original.

Rose Cottage is one of only two pieces sculpted in the coal shed in 1980 still current in 1994; the other is Market Street.

SCULPTED: 1980
LOCATION: The Coalshed
(remodelled at Hendon Road)
RELEASED: 1980 REMODELLED: 1983
SIZE: Width: 4 ½" Depth: 3" Height: 2 ¾"
MARKINGS: © DAVID WINTER
1980

MARKET STREET

The longest running David Winter Cottage, sculpted in mid-1980 and still available in stores fourteen years on. David cleverly derived two other models from this piece — The Winemerchant and Little Market — by cutting it in two and resculpting the join. Remodelling of Market Street was required in 1983 due to loss of detail in the moulds and the changes in detail were considerable.
Mould 1 The original had a name plaque ("MARKET STREET") but no other sculpted markings, no foliage, smaller chimneys not rising above roof level, a back door with horizontal and diagonal cross bars, a less distinct front cellar window, different beam patterns, overlapping roof crests at rear.
Mould 2 The remodelled version had the name plaque removed and copyright symbol, David's name and sculpture date added, foliage added, chimneys enlarged and protruding above roof level, cross bars on back

SCULPTED: 1980
LOCATION: The Coalshed
(remodelled at Hendon Road)
RELEASED: 1980 REMODELLED: 1983
SIZE: Width: 5 ½" Depth: 4" Height: 4 ½"
MARKINGS: Original - None: Remodelled -
© DAVID WINTER
1980

door removed, cellar window more prominent, top left window at rear positioned lower, all windows restyled, roof crests no longer overlapping.

TRIPLE OAST

Mould 1 The original was devoid of foliage and the white fencing. Roof tiles on early pieces were painted grey as opposed to the usual reddish brown. However the colour change was made before the piece was remodelled in 1985. *Mould 2* Foliage and white fencing were added. (See Single Oast entry which gives detailed changes made to both pieces.) Both versions are marked © DAVID WINTER as David omitted to add a date whilst remodelling.

SCULPTED: 1981
LOCATION: 19 Ash Street
(one of the first pieces sculpted there)
RELEASED:1981
REMODELLED: 1985
SIZE: Width: 7 ¼" Depth: 4 ⅝" Height: 5 ½"
MARKINGS: © DAVID WINTER

STRATFORD HOUSE

David Winter's first mature piece; he knew when he had finished sculpting Stratford House that he had, after eighteen months and more than twenty pieces, finally created a generic style for David Winter Cottages. It was a struggle and the form of Stratford House didn't come easily. John Hine recalls that at one time there was a stream running in front of it with a bridge which made it look lopsided. "David tried everything until finally a yell of 'eureka' from upstairs told us all that the sculptural problem had been solved. Once the proportions were right, everything fell into place." *(From the book 'Collecting David Winter Cottages.')* On early pieces there is a gap between the main house and the smaller house at left front. Then a foliage arch was added to make demoulding easier and to strengthen the piece, and eventually the gap was filled in completely. Stratford House was originally marked only with David's name; the copyright symbol and date were added at a later stage.

SCULPTED: 1981
LOCATION: 19 Ash Street
RELEASED: 1981
SIZE: Width: 6 ¼" Depth: 4" Height: 4 ⅝"
MARKINGS: DAVID WINTER / © DAVID WINTER 1981

Current Pieces

THE VILLAGE

Regarded by many as David's master-piece, The Village took three months to sculpt and was released as a special piece for Christmas 1981. *Mould 1* Watch out for colour variations on early pieces: John Hine's painters were given a free hand to interpret it in their own way prior to guidelines being established. Experiments with different types of paint were also being made at the time. Between 1981 and 1983 the production moulds gradually distorted, making the piece narrower along its length. The problem was then corrected. Also during this period, there were variations to the top of the chimney of the tall stone building at the front of the sculpture. The original shape, like a pyramid with the peak sliced off, was soon modified to ease demoulding; then it was changed back to David's initial design in 1983.

Mould 2 Three years later, The Village was taken out of production for eight months whilst numerous alterations were made, to eradicate demoulding difficulties and to prevent distortion. 1986 CHANGES: 1) Foliage added, especially numerous arches stretching between buildings to avoid mould distortion. 2) The stone building with the pyra-

SCULPTED: 1981
LOCATION: 19 Ash Street
(remodelled at Hendon Road)
RELEASED: 1981
REMODELLED: 1986
SIZE: Width: 12 1/4" Depth: 8" Height: 7 1/4"
MARKINGS: © DAVID WINTER 1981

mid chimney was made narrower by cutting the back away so it is flush with the chimney stack. 3) A buttress on the stone archway (to the right of the piece) was removed. 4) The building at left front was shortened by approximately half-an-inch, revealing more of the courtyard beyond.

DROVER'S COTTAGE

SCULPTED: 1982
LOCATION: Hendon Road
RELEASED: 1982
SIZE: Width: 3 1/8" Depth: 1 7/8" Height: 2 3/8"
MARKINGS: © DAVID WINTER 1982

SUSSEX COTTAGE

SCULPTED: 1982
LOCATION: Hendon Road
RELEASED: 1982
SIZE: Width: 3 1/2" Depth: 2 1/4" Height: 2 1/2"
MARKINGS: © DAVID WINTER 1982

THE VILLAGE SHOP

The date is missing from the base marking on early pieces. Unfortunately the wrong year (1983) was later added in error. Don't be deceived; the piece was sculpted and released in 1982. According to the shop sign, the proprietor's name is Askew, a delightful pun reflecting the building's crooked nature.

SCULPTED: 1982
LOCATION: Hendon Road
RELEASED: 1982
SIZE: Width: 2 7/8" Depth: 2" Height: 2 3/4"
MARKINGS: © DAVID WINTER /
© DAVID WINTER 1983

COTSWOLD COTTAGE

Originally the overhangs on the gables and porch were more prominent. They caused demoulding problems and were shortened in 1983.

SCULPTED: 1982
LOCATION: Hendon Road
RELEASED: 1982
SIZE: Width: 2 3/4" Depth: 2 1/2" Height: 2 1/8"
MARKINGS: © DAVID WINTER 1982

THE BAKEHOUSE

There was originally an extra band of bricks on the top of the chimney but only on very early models made in 1983. It was then removed.

SCULPTED: 1983
LOCATION: Home Studio
RELEASED: 1983
SIZE: Width: 3 1/2" Depth: 2 3/4" Height: 4"
MARKINGS: © DAVID WINTER 1983

THE BOTHY

SCULPTED: 1983
LOCATION: Home Studio
RELEASED: 1983
SIZE: Width: 4" Depth: 3 1/8"
Height: 3 5/8"
MARKINGS: © DAVID WINTER 1983

FISHERMAN'S WHARF

SCULPTED: 1983
LOCATION: Hendon Road
RELEASED: 1983
SIZE: Width: 4 ¹/₂" Depth: 3 ¹/₈"
Height: 3 ³/₄"
MARKINGS: © DAVID WINTER 1983

Early models do not have as much foliage, notably around the raised gable ends.

THE GREEN DRAGON INN

Sometimes called The Green Dragon Pub. Most models have a foliage arch at the top of the stairs, but this is missing on very early models. The pub sign was originally made of brown or black plastic, with a paper sign glued on. This was later changed to a more robust metal version with etching. To accommodate the new sign the foliage where it attaches to the model was extended for added strength.

SCULPTED: 1983
LOCATION: Hendon Road
RELEASED: 1983
SIZE: Width: 4 ¹/₂" Depth: 3 ³/₈"
Height: 3 ¹/₂"
MARKINGS: © DAVID WINTER 1983

THE PARSONAGE

Mould 1 David sculpted the original in a bedroom at his parents' house while an outhouse in his garden was being converted into a studio. The remodelling was done in the new studio; the changes involved two modifications a) cutting back the walls of the porch so they did not protrude as far (to prevent them from breaking off) and b) moving the small weather boarded building at front right half-an-inch nearer the main building (to ease demoulding). A beautiful customised Parsonage was specially painted by John Hine Studios master originator, Kerry Agar, as a charity raffle prize for CARNIVAL '93 at Warwick in October 1993. The winner was a collector from Exeter in Devon, England.

SCULPTED: 1984
LOCATION: David's parents' house.
RELEASED: 1984
REMODELLED: 1986
SIZE: Width: 9 ¹/₂" Depth: 7 ¹/₄" Height: 9"
MARKINGS: © DAVID WINTER 1984

KENT COTTAGE

David was driving through the Kent countryside with his friend and colleague Jonno Suart in late 1984 or early 1985 when he saw a dilapidated old cottage at the side of the road. (Neither can remember quite where it was, possibly near Deal or Folkestone.) They wandered around the house and took numerous photographs which David later used for reference as he sculpted Kent Cottage in his mother's studio.

SCULPTED: 1985
LOCATION: Faith Winter's Studio
RELEASED: 1985
SIZE: Width: 6 ³/₈" Depth: 3 ¹/₂" Height: 4 ¹/₈"
MARKINGS: © DAVID WINTER 1985

SCULPTED: 1986
LOCATION: Home Studio
RELEASED: 1987
SIZE: Width: 4" Depth: 4 ¹/₄" Height: 7 ¹/₈"
MARKINGS: © DAVID WINTER 1987

THERE WAS A CROOKED HOUSE

Inspired by the children's nursery rhyme and featuring all the items mentioned apart from the crooked man: *There was a crooked man and he walked a crooked mile, He found a crooked sixpence against a crooked stile; He bought a crooked cat, which caught a crooked mouse, And they all lived together in a little crooked house.* Audrey White's favourite piece, 'Crooked House' was sculpted in 1986 but not released until the following year. Look out for colour variations on the conical roof; the triangular sections on early pieces were painted green before being changed to grey. This is the only David Winter Cottage to feature a drainpipe!

Current Pieces

MOONLIGHT HAVEN

David says that he sculpted a piano on the outside of this piece to give John Hine something to write about! Consequently its working title became Piano Cottage but was changed before release to the more romantic Moonlight Haven. There is also the consideration that David sculpted the piece whilst listening to the recently recorded music for the video 'Meet The Artist' — hence the musical association. David intended Moonlight Haven to be a Guild exclusive but was persuaded that such a lovely sculpture should enter the main collection and be made available to all. Guild members benefited from this decision, however, as they got Will-'o-the-Wisp instead (Guild Piece No.10), regarded by many collectors as one of David's finest and underrated achievements.

SCULPTED: 1991
LOCATION: Home Studio
RELEASED: 1991
SIZE: Width: 5 ⁵/₈" Depth: 5 ¹/₂" Height: 5 ¹/₂"
MARKINGS: © DAVID WINTER 1991

CASTLE IN THE AIR

The points where the metal flags attach to the model were originally just Crystacal, but metal supports were then added for extra strength. The modification was made soon after the piece was released. At first the piece was supplied with only two metal cannons (which are not attached), but it is usually three. This *tour-de-force* was intended as a replacement for Falstaff's Manor, one of both David's and John's favourite pieces, when it retired in 1990/91. However, David got a bit carried away . . . and CASTLE IN THE AIR was the magnificent result.

SCULPTED: 1991
LOCATION: Home Studio
RELEASED: 1991
SIZE: Width: 6 ⁵/₈" Depth: 5 ⁵/₈" Height: 11"
MARKINGS: © DAVID WINTER 1991

INGLENOOK COTTAGE

SCULPTED: 1991
LOCATION: Home Studio
RELEASED: 1991
SIZE: Width: 3 $^1/_2$" Depth: 3 $^5/_8$" Height: 5"
MARKINGS: © DAVID WINTER 1991

THE WEAVER'S LODGINGS

SCULPTED: 1991
LOCATION: Home Studio
RELEASED: 1991
SIZE: Width: 3 $^3/_4$" Depth: 3 $^3/_8$" Height: 4 $^7/_8$"
MARKINGS: © DAVID WINTER 1991

HEART OF ENGLAND SERIES

THE APOTHECARY SHOP

SCULPTED: 1985
LOCATION: Home Studio
RELEASED: 1985
SIZE: Width: 4 $^1/_8$" Depth: 2" Height: 2 $^3/_4$"
MARKINGS: © D.W.C. 1985

Some early labels have a printing error —
The Apothercary Shop.

BLACKFRIARS GRANGE

SCULPTED: 1985
LOCATION: Home Studio
RELEASED: 1985
SIZE: Width: 3 $^1/_2$" Depth: 2 $^1/_8$" Height: 2 $^1/_2$"
MARKINGS: © D.W.C. 1985

CRAFTSMEN'S COTTAGES

SCULPTED: 1985
LOCATION: Home Studio
RELEASED: 1985
SIZE: Width: 4 ³/₄" Depth: 1 ⁷/₈" Height: 2 ¹/₂"
MARKINGS: © D.W.C. 1985

THE HOGS HEAD TAVERN

SCULPTED: 1985
LOCATION: Home Studio
RELEASED: 1985
SIZE: Width: 3 ³/₄" Depth: 2 ¹/₈" Height: 3"
MARKINGS: © D.W.C. 1985

The alternative name — The Hogs Head Beer House — is commonly found on backstamps. It may have been used for the fast developing North American market initially; however, 'Beer Houses' are also sold elsewhere, including the UK.

MEADOWBANK COTTAGES

SCULPTED: 1985
LOCATION: Home Studio
RELEASED: 1985
SIZE: Width: 4" Depth: 1 ³/₈" Height: 2 ¹/₄"
MARKINGS: © D.W.C. 1985

ST. GEORGE'S CHURCH

A model of David Winter's own village church, though given a different name.

SCULPTED: 1985
LOCATION: Home Studio
RELEASED: 1985
SIZE: Width: 4" Depth: 2 ¹/₄" Height: 3"
MARKINGS: © D.W.C. 1985

THE SCHOOLHOUSE

SCULPTED: 1985
LOCATION: Home Studio
RELEASED: 1985
SIZE: Width: 3 ¹/₂" Depth: 2 ¹/₂" Height: 2 ³/₄"
MARKINGS: © D.W.C. 1985

SHIREHALL

SCULPTED: 1985
LOCATION: Home Studio
RELEASED: 1985
SIZE: Width: 3 ¹/₂" Depth: 2" Height: 2 ³/₄"
MARKINGS: © D.W.C. 1985

THE VICARAGE

SCULPTED: 1985
LOCATION: Home Studio
RELEASED: 1985
SIZE: Width: 3 ⁷/₈" Depth: 2 ¹/₂" Height: 3"
MARKINGS: © D.W.C. 1985

YEOMAN'S FARMHOUSE

SCULPTED: 1985
LOCATION: Home Studio
RELEASED: 1985
SIZE: Width: 4 ¹/₈" Depth: 2" Height: 2 ¹/₈"
MARKINGS: © D.W.C. 1985

THE WINDMILL

The first of the Heart of England pieces to be sculpted but the last to be released. It took three years to develop the sails for The Windmill; balsa wood was used on the prototype and the first but unsuccessful idea for production was to use injection moulded plastic. The final solution was to have the sails cast in metal. A few early pieces have only six frames per sail but the design was standardised soon after launch at seven frames per sail. Though the piece is still current in early '94, pieces with six frames per sail are very collectable. If you see one in a shop, buy it!

SCULPTED: 1985
LOCATION: Home Studio
RELEASED: 1988
SIZE: Width: 2 ¹/₄" Depth: 2 ⁷/₈" Height: 3 ¹/₂"
MARKINGS: © D.W.C. 1985

WEST COUNTRY COLLECTION

Launched as a five-piece collection in 1987, with Cornish Engine House and Cornish Harbour added in 1988. Orchard Cottage was retired in November 1991- see RETIRED PIECES listing for details.

DEVON COMBE

SCULPTED: 1986
LOCATION: Home Studio
RELEASED: 1987
SIZE: Width: 5 $^7/_8$" Depth: 4 $^3/_8$"
Height: 5"
MARKINGS: © DAVID WINTER 1986

DEVON CREAMERY

SCULPTED: 1986
LOCATION: Home Studio
RELEASED: 1987
SIZE: Width: 5 $^5/_8$" Depth: 4 $^1/_4$"
Height: 4 $^1/_2$"
MARKINGS: © DAVID WINTER 1986

SMUGGLER'S CREEK

S mugglers Creek gave David Winter the first of many awards for his work — the 1987 award for Best Collectible of the Show at the California Plate & Collectible Show in Pasadena, USA. A highly complex design, extremely difficult to make; consequently mould-makers had a variety of work-ing names for it, none printable here. The piece has been tipped for retirement on many occasions by deal-ers and collectors alike.

SCULPTED: 1986
LOCATION: Home Studio
RELEASED: 1987
SIZE: Width: 7 $^1/_2$" Depth: 5 $^1/_4$" Height: 9"
MARKINGS: © DAVID WINTER 1986

TAMAR COTTAGE

SCULPTED: 1986
LOCATION: Home Studio
RELEASED: 1987
SIZE: Width: 4 ½" Depth: 3 ½"
Height: 5"
MARKINGS: © DAVID WINTER
1986

CORNISH ENGINE HOUSE

A remodelling of the earlier Cornish Tin Mine. The balcony and working pump wheel is all one metal attachment.

SCULPTED: 1987
LOCATION: Home Studio
RELEASED: 1988
SIZE: Width: 5 ¾" Depth: 3 ⅝"
Height: 7 ¼"
MARKINGS: © DAVID WINTER
1987

CORNISH HARBOUR

SCULPTED: 1987
LOCATION: Home
Studio
RELEASED: 1988
SIZE: Width: 5 ¾"
Depth: 5 ½"
Height: 6 ¼"
MARKINGS: © DAVID
WINTER 1987

MIDLANDS COLLECTION

Originally there were six pieces in the Midland Collection — Bottle Kiln was retired in November 1991. See list of RETIRED PIECES for details.

GUNSMITHS

SCULPTED: 1987
LOCATION: Home Studio
RELEASED: 1988
SIZE: Width: 4" Depth: 3 ¹/₂" Height: 4 ³/₄"
MARKINGS: © DAVID WINTER 1987

DERBYSHIRE COTTON MILL

A remodelled version of the earlier Cotton Mill. The footbridge is a new feature, so are the ridges on the stack, and the main building has been extended and reworked.

SCULPTED: 1987
LOCATION: Home Studio
RELEASED: 1988
SIZE: Width: 7"
Depth: 4" Height: 8 ¹/₂"
MARKINGS: © DAVID WINTER 1987

LACEMAKERS

L acemaker's Cottage was the intended name, but 'Cottage' was disgarded early on. The winding bannister is a metal attachment, and difficult to fit precisely. For this reason Lacemakers is regularly rumoured for retirement. David Winter has a particular fondness for the piece and has been heard to remark that he wouldn't mind living in a cottage like this

SCULPTED: 1987
LOCATION: Home Studio
RELEASED: 1988
SIZE: Width: 4 ¹/₄" Depth: 4 ³/₄" Height: 6"
MARKINGS: © DAVID WINTER 1987

LOCK-KEEPER'S COTTAGE

SCULPTED: 1987
LOCATION: Home Studio
RELEASED: 1988
SIZE: Width: 5" Depth: 4 ½" Height: 3 ¼"
MARKINGS: © DAVID WINTER 1987

Not a model of a real building but very similar to the handful of curious barrel-shaped cottages unique to a ten-mile stretch of canal stretching north from Stratford-Upon-Avon, Warwickshire. The cottages were built by the same navvies who built the canal network itself and one theory is that they made the roofs this shape because they were so used to constructing tunnels.

(COAL) MINERS ROW

Variations on the name abound — Miners Row, Coal Miners Row — but the piece was originally launched as Coalminers Row.

SCULPTED: 1987
LOCATION: Home Studio
RELEASED: 1988
SIZE: Width: 6 ¾" Depth: 4"
Height: 4 ¼"
MARKINGS: © DAVID WINTER 1987

SCOTTISH COLLECTION

The Old Distillery, originally sculpted in 1982, was relaunched without modification in 1989 as one of the Scottish Collection. It has since been retired (February 1993) — see RETIRED PIECES for details.

GATEKEEPERS

Gatekeepers normally has a grey roof, but a colourway edition of 1,000 was produced in 1991 — see section on Limited Edition Pieces.

SCULPTED: 1988
LOCATION: Home Studio
RELEASED: 1989
SIZE: Width: 4 ¼" Depth: 3 ⅛" Height: 5 ¼"
MARKINGS: © DAVID WINTER 1988

90

GILLIES COTTAGE

SCULPTED: 1988
LOCATION: Home Studio
RELEASED: 1989
SIZE: Width: 5" Depth: 4" Height: 4 1/4"
MARKINGS: © DAVID WINTER 1988

THE HOUSE ON THE LOCH

. . . And the Loch in question could only be Loch Ness! There's a monster's heading rising up from the murky depths.

SCULPTED: 1988
LOCATION: Home Studio
RELEASED: 1989
SIZE: Width: 4 5/8" Depth: 4 1/2" Height: 4"
MARKINGS: © DAVID WINTER 1988

MACBETH'S CASTLE

The evil character of Shakespeare's famous play is not the MacBeth who inhabits David's castle — inspiration came instead from the real MacBeth who ruled Scotland from AD1040 to 1057 and was, by all accounts, a kind and much-loved king. David used reference photographs of several Scottish castle whilst sculpting MacBeth's Castle, notably Cawdor Castle near Inverness, which has associations with the Shakespeare play.

SCULPTED: 1988
LOCATION: Home Studio
RELEASED: 1989
SIZE: Width: 5 1/2" Depth: 4 1/2" Height: 8 1/2"
MARKINGS: © DAVID WINTER 1988

SCOTTISH CROFTERS

A slightly remodelled version of an earlier piece, Crofters Cottage, the only difference being the addition of ropes on the roof weighted down with stones — a feature David regretted omitting from the original. He took the launch of the Scottish Collection as an opportunity to make the change and it was not intended to alter the name of the piece. However, it became known as Scottish Crofters at John Hine Studios to distinguish it from the original, and gradually the name stuck. The base marking refers to the date when the original Crofters Cottage was sculpted — 1986.

SCULPTED: 1988
LOCATION: Home Studio
RELEASED: 1989
SIZE: Width: 6 ¾" Depth: 4" Height: 4 ¼"
MARKINGS: © DAVID WINTER
1986

BRITISH TRADITIONS

A collection of twelve pieces inspired by famous (and not so famous) traditions of the British Isles — one for each month of the year.

BURNS' READING ROOM

SCULPTED: 1989
LOCATION: Home Studio
RELEASED: 1990
SIZE: Width: 3 ¼" Depth: 2" Height: 3 ¼"
MARKINGS: © D.W.C.
1989

MONTH AND TRADITION: January — Burns' Night. 25th January is Burns' Night when Scotland celebrates the birthday of its greatest poet, Robert Burns. Burns Reading Room is inspired by a painting by Henry G. Guiguid called 'William Smellie's Printing Office, Anchor Close, Edinburgh'. Smellie published some of Burns' work and the poet used to come here to proof read his poems. The building no longer exists, but the painting can be seen in the Prints & Drawing Room of the National Gallery of Scotland, Edinburgh.

STONECUTTER'S COTTAGE

MONTH AND TRADITION: February — Annual Meeting of the Ancient Order of Purbeck Marblers and Stonecutters. Distinctive Purbeck stone can be seen in cathedrals and other great buildings throughout Britain and the marblers and stone-cutters who provide it have held their annual meeting in the Town Hall, Corfe Castle, Dorset for nigh on a thousand years. David Winter's research assistant, Anne Le Butt, came across this obscure but fascinating tradition and Stonecutter's Cottage is based on a real cottage in the village of Worth Maltravers, a few miles from Corfe Castle.

SCULPTED: 1989
LOCATION: Home Studio
RELEASED: 1990
SIZE: Width: 4 ¹/₂" Depth: 3 ¹/₄" Height: 4 ¹/₂"
MARKINGS: © D.W.C.
1989

SCULPTED: 1989
LOCATION: Home Studio
RELEASED: 1990
SIZE: Width: 3 ⁷/₈" Depth: 2 ³/₄" Height: 4 ³/₈"
MARKINGS: © D.W.C.
1989

THE BOAT HOUSE

MONTH AND TRADITION: March — Oxford and Cambridge Boat Race; the annual race between students from England's finest universities held on a stretch of the River Thames in West London. *Mould 1* The Boat House has a variation to the thin rim of bricks around the top edges of the chimney. On the original version, produced between June 1989 and May 1990, the bricks are sharply-defined on both the inside and outside. *Mould 2* From May 1990 onwards, a bevel was added to the inside, sloping on all sides towards the centre. The change was made to prevent the rim from snapping off during demoulding. The Boat House also has a thick wooden post to the front of the piece which initially caused some production problems. A cut (known as a 'shim') had to be made in the mould in order to demould the post intact and it was changed from a vertical to a diagonal cut several times. The shim sometimes leaves a feint ridge across the stone floor close to the post and collectors who compare a number of pieces may notice that its position varies.

SCULPTED: 1989
LOCATION: Home Studio
RELEASED: 1990
SIZE: Width: 3 5/8" Depth: 3 3/8" Height: 5 1/4"
MARKINGS: © D.W.C. 1989

PUDDING COTTAGE

MONTH AND TRADITION: April —
Addlethwaite Yorkshire Pudding Festival. This
tradition is so obscure that no one has ever
heard of it, probably because it takes place
on 1st April when most people's attention is
centred on the more popular antics of April
Fool's Day. But yes, folks, Yorkshire Puddings
do grow on bushes and there's one meander-
ing its way up the side of Pudding Cottage to
prove it. (If you believe that, you'll believe
anything.)

BLOSSOM COTTAGE

SCULPTED: 1989
LOCATION: Home Studio
RELEASED: 1990
SIZE: Width: 4" Depth: 3 5/8" Height: 4 1/2"
MARKINGS: © D.W.C 1989

MONTH AND TRADITION: May — Chelsea
Flower Show. The home of a keen gardener
who wouldn't miss the greatest flower show
in the world for all the tea in Christendom.
The David Winter Toby Jug (see Memorabilia
section) features David Winter sitting on
Blossom Cottage, although the chimney had
to be moved slightly to one side . . . for
obvious reasons of
comfort!

KNIGHT'S CASTLE

SCULPTED: 1989
LOCATION: Home Studio
RELEASED: 1990
SIZE: Width: 3 3/8" Depth: 3 1/4" Height: 6"
MARKINGS: © D.W.C. 1989

*MONTH AND
TRADITION:*
June — Garter
Day Ceremony,
an annual pro-
cession held
at Windsor
Castle featur-
ing Her
Majesty The
Queen and her
twenty five
Knights of the
The Most Noble
Order of The
Garter.

Current Pieces

ST ANNE'S WELL

MONTH AND TRADITION: July — Well Dressing. St Anne is the Patron Saint of Wells and in Derbyshire they maintain the ancient summer tradition of adorning wells with colourful pictures made from flower heads and other foliage.

SCULPTED: 1989
LOCATION: Home Studio
RELEASED: 1990
SIZE: Width: 4 1/4" Depth: 3 1/4" Height: 4 5/8"
MARKINGS: © D.W.C. 1989

GROUSE MOOR LODGE

MONTH AND TRADITION: August — The Glorious Twelfth. 12th August marks the start of the grouse shooting season in Scotland and Northern England. Not so glorious if you happen to be a grouse.

SCULPTED: 1989
LOCATION: Home Studio
RELEASED: 1990
SIZE: Width: 3 1/8" Depth: 2 7/8"
Height: 4 3/4"
MARKINGS: © D.W.C. 1989

STAFFORDSHIRE VICARAGE

MONTH AND TRADITION: September — Abbots Bromley Horn Dance. A thousand year old tradition in which men from the Staffordshire village of Abbots Bromley dance around wearing reindeer antlers. They begin on the vicarage lawn, hence the sculpture.

SCULPTED: 1989
LOCATION: Home Studio
RELEASED: 1990
SIZE: Width: 4 1/4"
Depth: 3" Height: 4"
MARKINGS: © D.W.C. 1989

HARVEST BARN

MONTH AND TRADITION: October — Harvest Festival. The barn, scene of a supper and celebrations to mark the safe gathering in of the harvest — a tradition in many other countries and not just Britain.

SCULPTED: 1989
LOCATION: Home Studio
RELEASED: 1990
SIZE: Width: 4" Depth: 2 $\frac{1}{2}$" Height: 2 $\frac{1}{2}$"
MARKINGS: © D.W.C.
1989

GUY FAWKES

MONTH AND TRADITION: November — Bonfire Night. 5th November, the night when Britons celebrate the failed attempt to blow up King James VI and his entire Parliament in 1605. David's piece is based on drawings of the old House of Lords — demolished in the early nineteenth century — which was the very building Guy Fawkes and his co-conspirators targeted for their Gunpowder Plot.

SCULPTED: 1989
LOCATION: Home Studio
RELEASED: 1990
SIZE: Width: 2 $\frac{3}{4}$"
Depth: 2 $\frac{1}{2}$" Height: 3 $\frac{1}{4}$"
MARKINGS: © D.W.C.
1989

THE BULL AND BUSH

MONTH AND TRADITION: December — Pantomime. The Christmas and New Year tradition of pantomime has its routes in musical halls and pubs. 'Down at The Old Bull and Bush' is one of the most famous songs of this era and David sculpted his interpretation of the pub that inspired it. (The real one is in North London, between Hampstead Heath and Golders Green).

SCULPTED: 1989
LOCATION: Home Studio
RELEASED: 1990
SIZE: Width: 4 $\frac{1}{8}$"
Depth: 2 $\frac{1}{2}$" Height: 4"
MARKINGS: © D.W.C.
1989

CAMEOS

BARLEY MALT KILN

SCULPTED: 1991
LOCATION: Home Studio
RELEASED: 1992
SIZE: Width: 1 $^3/_4$" Depth: 1 $^5/_8$" Height: 1 ^{3},
MARKINGS: © D.W.C. 1991

BROOKLET BRIDGE

SCULPTED: 1991
LOCATION: Home Studio
RELEASED: 1992
SIZE: Width: 1 $^7/_8$" Depth: 1 $^3/_4$" Height: 1 $^1/_2$"
MARKINGS: © D.W.C. 1991

GREENWOOD WAGON

SCULPTED: 1991
LOCATION: Home Studio
RELEASED: 1992
SIZE: Width: 1 $^1/_2$" Depth: 1 $^5/_8$" Height: 1 $^1/_2$"
MARKINGS: © D.W.C. 1991

LYCH GATE

SCULPTED: 1991
LOCATION: Home Studio
RELEASED: 1992
SIZE: Width: 1 $^5/_8$" Depth: 1 $^1/_2$" Height: 1 $^5/_8$"
MARKINGS: © D.W.C. 1991

MARKET DAY

SCULPTED: 1991
LOCATION: Home Studio
RELEASED: 1992
SIZE: Width: 1 $^3/_4$" Depth: 1 $^5/_8$" Height: 1 $^1/_2$"
MARKINGS: © D.W.C. 1991

ONE MAN JAIL

SCULPTED: 1991
LOCATION: Home Studio
RELEASED: 1992
SIZE: Width: 1 $^3/_4$" Depth: 1 $^3/_4$" Height: 1 $^5/_8$"
MARKINGS: © D.W.C. 1991

PENNY WISHING WELL

SCULPTED: 1991
LOCATION: Home Studio
RELEASED: 1992
SIZE: Width: 1 ⁵/₈" Depth: 1 ³/₄" Height: 1 ⁵/₈"
MARKINGS: © D.W.C. 1991

THE POTTING SHED

SCULPTED: 1991
LOCATION: Home Studio
RELEASED: 1992
SIZE: Width: 1 ⁵/₈" Depth: 1 ³/₄" Height: 1 ³/₄"
MARKINGS: © D.W.C. 1991

POULTRY ARK

SCULPTED: 1991
LOCATION: Home Studio
RELEASED: 1992
SIZE: Width: 1 ⁵/₈" Depth: 1 ³/₈" Height: 1 ¹/₂"
MARKINGS: © D.W.C. 1991

THE PRIVY

SCULPTED: 1991
LOCATION: Home Studio
RELEASED: 1992
SIZE: Width: 1 ⁵/₈" Depth: 1 ³/₈" Height: 1 ⁷/₈"
MARKINGS: © D.W.C. 1991

SADDLE STEPS

SCULPTED: 1991
LOCATION: Home Studio
RELEASED: 1992
SIZE: Width: 1 ³/₄" Depth: 1 ¹/₂" Height: 1 ¹/₄"
MARKINGS: © D.W.C. 1991

WELSH PIG PEN

SCULPTED: 1991
LOCATION: Home Studio
RELEASED: 1992
SIZE: Width: 2" Depth: 1 ³/₈" Height: 1"
MARKINGS: © D.W.C. 1991

DIORAMA

SCULPTED: 1991
LOCATION: Home Studio
RELEASED: 1992
SIZE: Width: 13 ¹/₈"
Depth: 7 ⁹/₁₆" Height: 2"
MARKINGS: © D.W.C. 1991

Alightly painted version of the diorama was retired after only a few months in March 1992

IRISH COLLECTION

Secret Shebeen and Only A Span Apart were also part of the Irish Collection until their retirement in July 1993 — see RETIRED PIECES for details. Murphy and O'Donovan's Castle were later additions.

IRISH ROUND TOWER

SCULPTED: 1990/91
LOCATION: Home Studio and Ireland
RELEASED: 1991
SIZE: Width: 5" Depth: 3 ³/₄" Height: 4 ¹/₄"
MARKINGS: © DAVID WINTER 1991

FOGARTYS

SCULPTED: 1990/91
LOCATION: Home Studio and Ireland
RELEASED: 1990
SIZE: Width: 5 ¹/₂" Depth: 3 ³/₄" Height: 3 ⁷/₈"
MARKINGS: © DAVID WINTER 1991

MURPHYS

SCULPTED: 1992
LOCATION: Home Studio and Ireland
RELEASED: 1992
SIZE: Width: 4 ¼" Depth: 3 ¼" Height: 5 ¾"
MARKINGS: © DAVID WINTER 1992

O'DONOVAN'S CASTLE

SCULPTED: 1992
LOCATION: Home Studio
and Ireland
RELEASED: 1992
SIZE: Width: 6 ½"
Depth: 4 ⅞" Height: 7"
MARKINGS:
© **DAVID WINTER 1992**

THE SHIRES

BERKSHIRE MILKING BYRE

Approximately one month into production, the bottom row of tiles on the outbuilding on the right was thickened to prevent damage during demoulding.

SCULPTED: 1992
LOCATION: Home Studio
RELEASED: 1993
SIZE: Width: 3 ⅜" Depth: 2 ⅛" Height: 2 ⅜"
MARKINGS: © DAVID WINTER 1992

BUCKINGHAMSHIRE BULL PEN

SCULPTED: 1992
LOCATION: Home Studio
RELEASED: 1993
SIZE: Width: 3" Depth: 2 ½" Height: 2"
MARKINGS: © DAVID WINTER 1992

100

CHESHIRE KENNELS

SCULPTED: 1992
LOCATION: Home Studio
RELEASED: 1993
SIZE: Width: 2 $^{7}/_{8}$" Depth: 2 $^{1}/_{8}$" Height: 2"
MARKINGS: © DAVID WINTER 1992

DERBYSHIRE DOVECOTE

SCULPTED: 1992
LOCATION: Home Studio
RELEASED: 1993
SIZE: Width: 2 $^{5}/_{8}$" Depth: 1 $^{5}/_{8}$" Height: 2 $^{3}/_{4}$"
MARKINGS: © DAVID WINTER 1992

GLOUCESTERSHIRE GREENHOUSE

SCULPTED: 1992
LOCATION: Home Studio
RELEASED: 1993
SIZE: Width: 3 $^{1}/_{8}$" Depth: 2 $^{3}/_{8}$" Height: 2 $^{1}/_{8}$"
MARKINGS: © DAVID WINTER 1992

HAMPSHIRE HUTCHES

SCULPTED: 1992
LOCATION: Home Studio
RELEASED: 1993
SIZE: Width: 2 $^{3}/_{4}$" Depth: 1 $^{3}/_{4}$" Height: 2 $^{5}/_{8}$"
MARKINGS: © DAVID WINTER 1992

LANCASHIRE DONKEY SHED

SCULPTED: 1992
LOCATION: Home Studio
RELEASED: 1993
SIZE: Width: 2 $^{3}/_{4}$" Depth: 3 $^{1}/_{4}$" Height: 2 $^{5}/_{8}$"
MARKINGS: © DAVID WINTER 1992

OXFORDSHIRE GOAT YARD

SCULPTED: 1992
LOCATION: Home Studio
RELEASED: 1993
SIZE: Width: 3" Depth: 2 $^1/_4$" Height: 2 $^5/_8$"
MARKINGS: © DAVID WINTER 1992

SHROPSHIRE PIG SHELTER

SCULPTED: 1992
LOCATION: Home Studio
RELEASED: 1993
SIZE: Width: 2 $^5/_8$" Depth: 2 $^1/_2$" Height: 2 $^3/_4$"
MARKINGS: © DAVID WINTER 1992

STAFFORDSHIRE STABLE

SCULPTED: 1992
LOCATION: Home Studio
RELEASED: 1993
SIZE: Width: 3" Depth: 2" Height: 2 $^1/_2$"
MARKINGS: © DAVID WINTER 1992

WILTSHIRE WATER-WHEEL

SCULPTED: 1992
LOCATION: Home Studio
RELEASED: 1993
SIZE: Width: 3" Depth: 2 $^1/_4$" Height: 2 $^5/_8$"
MARKINGS: © DAVID WINTER 1992

YORKSHIRE SHEEP FOLD

SCULPTED: 1992
LOCATION: Home Studio
RELEASED: 1993
SIZE: Width: 2 $^3/_4$" Depth: 2 $^1/_4$" Height: 2 $^1/_8$"
MARKINGS: © DAVID WINTER 1992

SCENES

The vignette bases only are by David Winter. The hand-cast bronze figures are by Cameo Guild Inc.

AT THE BOTHY

SCULPTED: 1992
LOCATION: Home Studio
RELEASED: 1993
SIZE: Width: 4" Depth: 3"
Height: 1 $^1/_2$"
MARKINGS: © DAVID WINTER 1992

AT THE BAKEHOUSE

SCULPTED: 1992
LOCATION: Home Studio
RELEASED: 1993
SIZE: Width: 4" Depth: 3"
Height: 1 $^3/_8$"
MARKINGS: © DAVID WINTER 1992

AT ROSE COTTAGE

SCULPTED: 1992
LOCATION: Home Studio
RELEASED: 1993
SIZE: Width: 3 $^3/_4$" Depth: 2 $^1/_2$"
Height: 1 $^7/_8$"
MARKINGS: © DAVID WINTER 1992

CHRISTMAS SCENE

SCULPTED: 1992
LOCATION: Home Studio
RELEASED: 1993
SIZE: Width: 4 $^3/_4$" Depth: 4 $^1/_2$"
Height: 1 $^1/_2$"
MARKINGS: © DAVID WINTER 1992

WELSH COLLECTION

All four titles are in the Welsh language.

Y DDRAIG GOCH

Originally to be called EICH DYN. See section on Rare and Unreleased Pieces. Y Ddraig Goch means 'The Red Dragon.'

SCULPTED: 1993
LOCATION: Home Studio
RELEASED: 1993
SIZE: Width: 6 ¼" Depth: 3 ⅛" Height: 4"
MARKINGS: © DAVID WINTER 1993

PEN-Y-GRAIG

Pen-y-Graig means 'Head of the Rock.'

SCULPTED: 1993
LOCATION: Home Studio
RELEASED: 1993
SIZE: Width: 4 ⅝" Depth: 4 ⅜"
Height: 4 ⅞"
MARKINGS: © DAVID WINTER 1993

Current Pieces

TYDDYN SYRIOL

Tyddyn Syriol means 'Cheerful Homestead.'

SCULPTED: 1993
LOCATION: Home Studio
RELEASED: 1993
SIZE: Width: 4 ⁷/₈" Depth: 3 ³/₄" Height: 3 ¹/₄"
MARKINGS: © DAVID WINTER 1993

LLANFAIRPWLLGWYNGYLL-GOGERYCHWYRNDROBWLL-LLANTYSILIOGOGOGOCH
(A BIT OF NONSENSE)

SCULPTED: 1993
LOCATION: Home Studio
RELEASED: 1993
SIZE: Width: 9 ¹/₂" Depth: 2" Height: 3 ¹/₂"
MARKINGS: © DAVID WINTER 1993

Rough translation: 'St Mary's Church in the hollow of white hazel near the rushing whirlpool with the Church of Tysilio by the red cave.' Sculpted by David at John Hine's request as a joke. The village that boasts this 58-letter name is in Anglesey, North Wales. Incredibly, it is not the longest place name in the world — a village in New Zealand enjoys that claim to fame.

THE ENGLISH VILLAGE

1. THE HALL

SCULPTED: 1993
LOCATION: Home Studio
RELEASED: December 1993
SIZE: Width: 3 $\frac{7}{8}$" Depth: 2 $\frac{7}{8}$ " Height:3 $\frac{5}{8}$"
MARKINGS: © DAVID WINTER 1993

2. ONE ACRE COTTAGE

SCULPTED: 1993
LOCATION: Home Studio
RELEASED: December 1993
SIZE: Width: 3 $\frac{7}{8}$" Depth: 2 $\frac{3}{4}$ " Height:3 $\frac{5}{8}$"
MARKINGS: © DAVID WINTER 1993

3. THE SMITHY

SCULPTED: 1993
LOCATION: Home Studio
RELEASED: December 1993
SIZE: Width: 3 $\frac{3}{4}$" Depth: 2 $\frac{7}{8}$" Height: 3 $\frac{3}{8}$"
MARKINGS: © DAVID WINTER 1993

4. THE TANNERY

SCULPTED: 1993
LOCATION: Home Studio
RELEASED: December 1993
SIZE: Width: 3 $\frac{3}{4}$" Depth: 3 $\frac{7}{8}$" Height: 3 $\frac{1}{4}$"
MARKINGS: © DAVID WINTER 1993

5. THE RECTORY

SCULPTED: 1993
LOCATION: Home Studio
RELEASED: December 1993
SIZE: Width: 3 $\frac{1}{2}$" Depth: 3 $\frac{7}{8}$" Height: 3 $\frac{1}{2}$"
MARKINGS: © DAVID WINTER 1993

6. THE CHURCH AND VESTRY

SCULPTED: 1993
LOCATION: Home Studio
RELEASED: January 1994
SIZE: Width: 3 $\frac{1}{4}$" Depth: 2 $\frac{5}{8}$ " Height:3 $\frac{5}{8}$"
MARKINGS: © DAVID WINTER 1993

7. GLEBE COTTAGE

SCULPTED: 1993
LOCATION: Home Studio
RELEASED: January 1994
SIZE: Width: 3 $\frac{7}{8}$" Depth: 2 $\frac{1}{2}$ " Height:3 $\frac{1}{2}$"
MARKINGS: © DAVID WINTER 1993

8. THE QUACK'S COTTAGE

SCULPTED: 1993
LOCATION: Home Studio
RELEASED: January 1994
SIZE: Width: 3 $\frac{1}{4}$" Depth: 2 $\frac{5}{8}$ " Height:3 $\frac{5}{8}$"
MARKINGS: © DAVID WINTER 1993

9. THE 'CAT AND PIPE' INN

SCULPTED: 1993
LOCATION: Home Studio
RELEASED: January 1994
SIZE: Width: 3 $\frac{1}{2}$" Depth: 2 $\frac{7}{8}$ " Height:4"
MARKINGS: © DAVID WINTER 1993

10. THE CONSTABULARY

SCULPTED: 1993
LOCATION: Home Studio
RELEASED: January 1994
SIZE: Width: 3 $\frac{1}{4}$" Depth: 2 $\frac{1}{2}$ " Height:3 $\frac{7}{8}$"
MARKINGS: © DAVID WINTER 1993

10   6

9   7   8

11. THE SEMINARY

SCULPTED: 1993
LOCATION: Home Studio
RELEASED: July 1994
SIZE: Width: 3 ³/₈" Depth: 2 ³/₄ " Height:3 ³/₄"
MARKINGS: © DAVID WINTER 1993

12. THE CHANDLERY

SCULPTED: 1993
LOCATION: Home Studio
RELEASED: July 1994
SIZE: Width: 3" Depth: 2 ⁵/₈ " Height:3 ³/₄"
MARKINGS: © DAVID WINTER 1993

13. CRYSTAL COTTAGE

SCULPTED: 1993
LOCATION: Home Studio
RELEASED: July 1994
SIZE: Width: 3 ¹/₄" Depth: 2 ¹/₂ " Height:3 ¹/₂"
MARKINGS: © DAVID WINTER 1993

14. THE POST OFFICE

SCULPTED: 1993
LOCATION: Home Studio
RELEASED: July 1994
SIZE: Width: 3 ³/₄" Depth: 2 ⁵/₈ " Height:3 ⁷/₈"
MARKINGS: © DAVID WINTER 1993

15. THE ENGINE HOUSE

SCULPTED: 1993
LOCATION: Home Studio
RELEASED: December 1993 — Walt Disney
World, Florida: January 1995 — Worldwide.
SIZE: Width: 3 ³/₈" Depth: 2 ⁵/₈ " Height:4 ³/₁₆"
MARKINGS: © DAVID WINTER 1993

The Engine House was launched in December 1993 at Walt Disney World in Florida to commemorate David Winter's Christmas visit, and remains available exclusively from Walt Disney World throughout 1994. The piece will join the current range and become generally available in January 1995, with painting modifications and a base disc instead of a conventional label.

New Additions to the Range

Here is some space to help keep up-to-date with new pieces.

NAME OF PIECE:
DATE OF ISSUE:
SIZE:
ISSUE PRICE:
OTHER INFORMATION:

NAME OF PIECE:
DATE OF ISSUE:
SIZE:
ISSUE PRICE:
OTHER INFORMATION:

NAME OF PIECE:
DATE OF ISSUE:
SIZE:
ISSUE PRICE:
OTHER INFORMATION:

NAME OF PIECE:
DATE OF ISSUE:
SIZE:
ISSUE PRICE:
OTHER INFORMATION:

NAME OF PIECE:
DATE OF ISSUE:
SIZE:
ISSUE PRICE:
OTHER INFORMATION:

NAME OF PIECE:
DATE OF ISSUE:
SIZE:
ISSUE PRICE:
OTHER INFORMATION:

NAME OF PIECE:
DATE OF ISSUE:
SIZE:
ISSUE PRICE:
OTHER INFORMATION:

Notes

Notes

Special Pieces for the David Winter Cottages Collectors Guild

The David Winter Cottages Collectors Guild was established in 1987 to offer collectors information and special pieces available exclusively to Guild members. The information comes in the form of a quarterly magazine, *Cottage Country*, and there have so far been three special pieces every year — a free membership piece and two 'redemption' pieces which members have the option to purchase.

The redemption pieces are highly collectable. Edition sizes are generally low, being determined not just by the number of Guild members but by the number who place an order (in the region of 50% of the total membership). Membership pieces have a larger edition size but are a worthwhile investment for free, and in some years have proved to be exceptional value, such as the 1989 Bas-Relief Plaque.

VILGE SCENE

The first complementary Guild piece, offered for members who joined in 1987 and 1988. A modified version of an existing stockist point-of-sale, the words 'Collectors Guild' were added onto the oval plaque beneath 'David Winter Cottages.'

SCULPTED: 1986
LOCATION: Home Studio
RELEASED: 1986/7 RETIRED: 1988
SIZE: Width: 4 3/4" Depth: 1 3/8" Height: 7 3/8"
MARKINGS: None
ISSUE PRICE: £0 $0

SCULPTED: 1986
LOCATION: Home Studio
RELEASED: 1987 RETIRED: 1989
SIZE: Width: 4 3/4" Depth: 4" Height: 4 3/8"
MARKINGS: GUILD NO.1
© DAVID WINTER SEPT 1986
ISSUE PRICE: £18 $54

ROBIN HOOD'S HIDEAWAY

The first 'redemption' piece available for purchase exclusively by Guild members.
Painting variations exist: a) Early models have a darker tree trunk; on later pieces it is silvery grey. b) Early pieces have red flowers, later ones blue and yellow. The change was instigated by Audrey White who pointed out that red flowers wouldn't grow so deep in a forest. The blue and yellows suggest bluebells and primroses. (Audrey knew a thing or two about flowers.) One of only three pieces marked with the month as well the date; the other two are Queen Elizabeth Slept Here and The Grange.

QUEEN ELIZABETH SLEPT HERE

The offer to purchase this splendid piece was not taken up by as many Guild members as you would imagine; they regarded it as too expensive at the time. The irony of this is that John Hine Studios had underpriced QESH having underestimated the painting time for the extensive beamwork. It was actually a bargain.

SCULPTED: 1987
LOCATION: Home Studio
RELEASED: 1987 RETIRED: 1989
SIZE: Width: 8" Depth: 5 ³/₄" Height: 6 ¹/₂"
MARKINGS: GUILD NO.2
© DAVID WINTER MAY 1987
ISSUE PRICE: £70 $183

BLACK BESS INN

A piece inspired by the exploits of ace highwayman Dick Turpin, Black Bess being his legendary horse. One of Turpin's stamping grounds, research reveals, was the main runway of Heathrow Airport (remote heathland at the time).

SCULPTED: 1988
LOCATION: Home Studio
RELEASED: 1988 RETIRED: 1990
SIZE: Width: 5 ⁵/₈" Depth: 4 ³/₈" Height: 5"
MARKINGS: GUILD NO.3
©DAVID WINTER 1988
ISSUE PRICE: £25 $60

THE PAVILION

Spelling variations exist on the backstamp and labels — The Pavillion, with two 'l's is commonly found.

SCULPTED: 1988
LOCATION: Home Studio
RELEASED: 1988 RETIRED: 1990
SIZE: Width: 5 ³/₈" Depth: 3 ³/₄" Height: 4 ¹/₂"
MARKINGS: GUILD NO.4
© DAVID WINTER 1988
ISSUE PRICE: £23 $52

SCULPTED: 1989
LOCATION: Home Studio
RELEASED: 1989 RETIRED: December 1989
SIZE: Diameter: 8 ¼" Depth: 1 ¼"
MARKINGS: © DAVID WINTER 1989
ISSUE PRICE: £0 $0

STREET SCENE (Bas-Relief Plaque)

David's first bas-relief plaque, offered as a complementary piece for the 1989 Guild. Getting the perspective right was a technical challenge for David and an enjoyable contrast from three-dimensional cottages. Originally the piece was called simply 'Bas-Relief Plaque', and the name Street Scene came later.

HOME GUARD

SCULPTED: 1988
LOCATION: Home Studio
RELEASED: 1989 RETIRED: 1991
SIZE: Width: 5 ¾" Depth: 4 ¾" Height: 4 ¾"
MARKINGS: GUILD NO.5
© DAVID WINTER 1988
ISSUE PRICE: £46 $105

Sculpted to commemorate the 50th anniversary of the outbreak of World War II and as a tribute to the real Dad's Army. John Hine suggested the idea during a pub meeting and David was so enthused by the subject that he completed sculpting Home Guard in just a few days.

THE COAL SHED

SCULPTED: 1989
LOCATION: Home Studio
RELEASED: 1989 RETIRED: 1991
SIZE: Width: 7 ¾" Depth: 4 ¼" Height: 4 ½"
MARKINGS: GUILD NO.6
© DAVID WINTER 1989
ISSUE PRICE: £50 $112

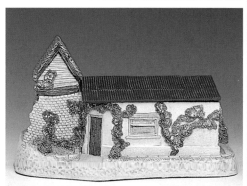

A model of the coalshed in which the first David Winter Cottages were made, sculpted to commemorate the 10th anniversary of John and David's partnership. The metal roof is removable and two figures can be seen inside, David sitting sculpting and John talking on a wall telephone. Find the words OXO and you should see (half) a mouse!

THE PLUCKED DUCKS

A flat-backed bas-relief plaque in a rectangular shadow box — the complementary gift for 1990 Guild members.

SCULPTED: 1989
LOCATION: Home Studio
RELEASED: 1990 RETIRED: December 1990
SIZE: Width: 7" Height: 5 ¼"
MARKINGS: © DAVID WINTER 1989
ISSUE PRICE: £0 $0

THE COBBLER

B ecause the 1990 Guild redemption pieces (The Cobbler and The Pottery) were smaller than in previous years they did not excite as much interest with collectors at the time. The excitement has come years on, with the secondary market recognising their (relative) rarity value.

SCULPTED: 1989
LOCATION: Home Studio
RELEASED: 1990 RETIRED: 1992
SIZE: Width: 2 ⅝" Depth: 2 ½" Height: 3"
MARKINGS: GUILD NO. 7
© DAVID WINTER 1989
ISSUE PRICE: £15 $40

THE POTTERY

See The Cobbler.

SCULPTED: 1989
LOCATION: Home Studio
RELEASED: 1990 RETIRED: 1992
SIZE: Width: 3 ½" Depth: 2" Height: 2 ¾"
MARKINGS: GUILD NO.8
© DAVID WINTER 1989
ISSUE PRICE: £15 $40

PERSHORE MILL

SCULPTED: 1990
LOCATION: Home Studio
RELEASED: 1991 RETIRED: December 1991
SIZE: Width: 7" Depth: Height: 5 1/4"
MARKINGS: © DAVID WINTER 1990
ISSUE PRICE: £0 $0

Similar to The Plucked Ducks, a flat-backed bas-relief plaque in a shadow box (this time hexagonal) — the complementary gift for 1991 Guild members. There was a real mill in Pershore, Worcestershire — John Hine grew up in that part of the world and knew it well. But it no longer exists and David's piece is entirely imaginary. So too are the antics in John's remarkable book *The Tale of Pershore Mill*, inspired by David's sculpture. He also wrote a song to promote the book — *The Maids of Pershore Mill*.

TOMFOOL'S COTTAGE

A piece inspired by the legend of the so-called 'wise' men of Gotham, near Nottingham, who pretended to be fools to prevent King John from . . . oh it's a long story!

WILL-'O-THE-WISP

An enigmatic title for a lovely piece, regarded highly by collectors.

SCULPTED: 1990
LOCATION: Home Studio
RELEASED: 1991 RETIRED: 1992
SIZE: Width: 4 3/4" Depth: 4 1/8" Height: 5 1/4"
MARKINGS: GUILD NO.9
© DAVID WINTER 1990
ISSUE PRICE: £35 $100

SCULPTED: 1991
LOCATION: Home Studio
RELEASED: 1991 RETIRED: 1992
SIZE: Width: 6 1/2" Depth: 3 1/2" Height: 6 1/4"
MARKINGS: GUILD NO.10
© DAVID WINTER 1991
ISSUE PRICE: £55 $120

SCULPTED: 1991
LOCATION: Home Studio
RELEASED: 1992 RETIRED: December 1992
SIZE: Width: 3 $^7/_8$" Depth: 2 $^7/_8$" Height: 2 $^5/_8$"
MARKINGS: © DAVID WINTER 1991
ISSUE PRICE: £0 $0

IRISH WATER MILL

Early pieces were delivered to stores with the incorrect working title 'Patrick's Water Mill' on the back-stamp and box labels. Irish Water Mill was the complementary gift for 1992 Guild members.

THE BEEKEEPER'S

Supplied with a small jar of English honey.

SCULPTED: 1991
LOCATION: Home Studio
RELEASED: 1992 RETIRED: December 1992
SIZE: Width: 3" Depth: 2 $^3/_4$" Height: 5 $^3/_4$"
MARKINGS: GUILD NO 11
© DAVID WINTER 1991
ISSUE PRICE: £34 $65

THE CANDLEMAKER'S

Supplied with a small candle made from British beeswax.

SCULPTED: 1991
LOCATION: Home Studio
RELEASED: 1992 RETIRED: December 1992
SIZE: Width: 4 $^1/_8$" Depth: 3 $^1/_2$" Height: 4 $^3/_8$"
MARKINGS: GUILD NO 12
© DAVID WINTER 1991
ISSUE PRICE: £34 $65

ON THE RIVERBANK

SCULPTED: 1992
LOCATION: Home Studio
RELEASED: 1993 RETIRED: December 1993
SIZE: Diameter: 8 ½" Depth: 1 ½"
MARKINGS: © DAVID WINTER 1992
ISSUE PRICE: £0 $0

A bas-relief plaque similar in dimensions to Street Scene but depicting a very different subject matter. features numerous animals including a fish, a fox-like dog (or dog-like fox, if you prefer), an owl (flying away) and a mouse.

THAMESIDE

A ttempts to supply this piece together with a small bottle of Thames river water were thwarted by health and safety regulations, so a solid crystacal bottle marked 'Not River Thames Water' took its place.

SCULPTED: 1992
LOCATION: Home Studio
RELEASED: 1993 RETIRED: December 1993
SIZE: Width: 3 ½" Depth: 3 ¼" Height: 5 ½"
MARKINGS: © DAVID WINTER 1992
ISSUE PRICE: £40 $79

SWAN UPPING COTTAGE

S upplied with a minia-ture model of a swan, sculpted by Matthew Luzny.

SCULPTED: 1992
LOCATION: Home Studio
RELEASED: 1993 RETIRED: December 1993
SIZE: Width: 3 ¾" Depth: 3" Height: 5 ¼"
MARKINGS: © DAVID WINTER 1992
ISSUE PRICE: £35 $69

15 LAWNSIDE ROAD

SCULPTED: 1993
LOCATION: Home Studio
RELEASED: 1994
RETIREMENT DATE: December 1994
SIZE: Left Face: 3" Right Face: 2 3/4"
Height: 3 3/4"
MARKINGS: © DAVID WINTER 1993
ISSUE PRICE: £0 $0

Acorner piece, with two flat sides and an angled facade — rather like the Bookend pieces without the wooden surround. Inspired by the game of croquet (note game equipment on edge of lawn) and the complementary piece for 1994 Guild members. Initially the facade to the left was beamed like the right side, but this was rendered during pre-production and none was released to Guild members in the original style.

WHILEAWAY COTTAGE

SCULPTED: 1993
LOCATION: Home Studio
RELEASED: 1994
RETIREMENT DATE: December 1994
SIZE: Width: 4 1/8" Depth: 3 1/8" Height: 4"
MARKINGS: GUILD NO 15
© DAVID WINTER 1993
ISSUE PRICE: £40 $70

ASHE COTTAGE

Ashe is the maiden name of Faith Winter, David's mother.

SCULPTED: 1993
LOCATION: Home Studio
RELEASED: 1994
RETIREMENT DATE: December 1994
SIZE: Width: 4 1/4" Depth: 3 1/4" Height: 4 1/4"
MARKINGS: GUILD NO 16
© DAVID WINTER 1993
ISSUE PRICE: £35 $62

Limited Edition & Christmas Pieces

A number of pieces have been released by John Hine Studios intended specifically as limited editions though the edition size is not always known. They comprise the Christmas pieces, special event and charity pieces. The exceptions are Mad Baron Fourthrite's Folly and Horatio Pernickety's Amorous Intent, Plum Cottage and Guardian Castle. Others are bound to follow.

SCULPTED: 1993
RELEASED: April 1993 RETIRED: May 1993
EDITION SIZE: Unknown
SIZE: Width: 7 $\frac{5}{8}$" Depth: 4 $\frac{5}{8}$" Height: 6 $\frac{1}{4}$"
MARKINGS: © DAVID WINTER 1993
ISSUE PRICE: £N/A $150

ARCHES THRICE

A magnificent piece sculpted from scratch by David in less than two weeks and inspired by an illustration of London Bridge in the seventeenth century. Arches Thrice was available in USA and Canada during David's 1993 month-long North American tour, and only from the stores which he visited. The piece was not made available elsewhere worldwide.

BIRTH DAY COTTAGE
(Arches Thwonce)

SCULPTED: 1993
RELEASED: July 1993
RETIREMENT DATE: June 1994
EDITION SIZE: Unknown
SIZE: Width: 4 $\frac{1}{8}$" Depth: 3 $\frac{3}{8}$" Height: 3 $\frac{1}{2}$"
MARKINGS: © DAVID WINTER 1993
ISSUE PRICE: £25 $55

The 1993/1994 replacement for Birthstone Wishing Well (see next page), only available at in-store promotions and special events. Again each piece can be customised for a collector (a) by attaching two metal signs above the front door featuring the day and month of his/her birth and (b) by painting an initial onto the plaque next to the front door (two initials if the painter is clever). The sub-title Arches Thwonce was scribble onto the base of the wax master by David Winter as a joke (having completed Arches Thrice just prior to this piece).

BIRTHSTONE WISHING WELL

SCULPTED: 1992
RELEASED: July 1992
RETIRED: June 1993
EDITION SIZE: Unknown
SIZE: Width: 4 ¼" Depth: 2 ⅜" Height: 2 ⅞"
MARKINGS: © DAVID WINTER 1992
ISSUE PRICE: £25 $40

The first David Winter Cottage sculpted exclusively for promotions, available for purchase for one year only at in-store promotions and special events. At front right is a wishing well with two open covers. Whilst making a wish the collector purchasing the piece could place into the well a small gemstone appropriate to his or her month of birth. The well covers were then sealed. If the covers are never removed the wish will apparently come true (!?!). Each piece was also customised with the purchaser's initials, painted onto the thatched roof, back wall or chimney.

CARTWRIGHT'S COTTAGE

SCULPTED: 1988
RELEASED: 1990 RETIRED: 1990
EDITION SIZE: Unknown
SIZE: Width: 4" Depth: 2 ¾"
Height: 3 ½"
MARKINGS: © DAVID WINTER 1988
ISSUE PRICE: £35 $45

For two years Cartwright's Cottage sat patiently on a shelf at John Hine Studios awaiting release, during which time it firstly became known as 'Lynne' (after Lynne Kentish, a member of John Hine Studios for a number of years) and then 'Selfridges' (pending a possible special promotion at the London department store of that name). Eventually it found a home as a charity piece for North America to balance 'Wintershill'. Sale of the edition raised $235,000 for Ronald McDonald Children's Charities.

THE CASTLE COTTAGE OF WARWICK

Sculpted for and available exclusively in person from CARNIVAL '93, John Hine Studios' two day promotion held inside the grounds of Warwick Castle on 2nd and 3rd October 1993.

SCULPTED: 1993
RELEASED: 3rd October 1993
RETIRED: 4th October 1993
EDITION SIZE: Believed to be 4,000
SIZE: Width: 5 ¾" Depth: 4 ¾" Height: 8 ¾"
MARKINGS: © DAVID WINTER 1993
ISSUE PRICE: £99.95 $N\A

GATEKEEPERS COLOURWAY

A limited edition colourway of Gatekeeper's from the Scottish Collection, produced as a charity piece to raise money for Haylands Farm on the Isle of Wight. The piece was launched at the London Collectors Showcase, a two day show held in West London, October 1991, and pieces from the edition were still available from John Hine Studios during 1993. The normal production version of Gatekeeper's has grey roof tiles — on the colourway they are reddish-brown. Otherwise they are identical.

SCULPTED: 1988
RELEASED: October 1991
RETIRED: 1992/93 EDITION SIZE: 1,000
SIZE: Width: 4 1/4" Depth: 3 1/8" Height: 5 1/4"
MARKINGS: © DAVID WINTER 1988
ISSUE PRICE: £65 $N/A

HORATIO PERNICKETY'S AMOROUS INTENT

The sequel to Mad Baron Fourthrite's Folly, offered during April 1993 only and with priority to Guild members. This time the edition size of 9,990 (half that of the Mad Baron piece) was set in advance. In addition to the numbered edition, approximately 3,000 unnumbered pieces were made available to stores for display.

SCULPTED: 1992
RELEASED: 1st April 1993
RETIRED: 30th April 1993
EDITION SIZE: 9,990 (plus 3,000 unnumbered store samples)
SIZE: Width: 4 3/4" Depth: 4 1/2" Height: 7 1/2"
MARKINGS: © DAVID WINTER 1992
ISSUE PRICE: £175 $350

GUARDIAN CASTLE

SCULPTED: 1994
RELEASED: 15th July 1994 (USA) — September 1994 worldwide
EDITION SIZE:
SIZE: Width: 5 1/2" Depth: 5"
Height: 10 1/2"
MARKINGS: © DAVID WINTER 1994
ISSUE PRICE:

A castle to complete the English Village collection. The edition size and issue price had not been finalised when this book went to print.

Photograph courtesy of John Hine Ltd.

Limited Edition & Christmas Pieces

MAD BARON FOURTHRITE'S FOLLY

A Limited Time Edition piece. Orders for Mad Baron Fourthrite's Folly could be place for one month only during 1992. Pieces were then made to fulfil the orders, which amounted to 18,854. The backstamp of every piece was numbered. Metal figures representing Mad Baron and his wife Baroness Hardunbuy appear on the piece and the storyline that John Hine developed around their tempestuous relationship spawned a stage show, a video, a cassette tape and two booklets.

SCULPTED: 1992
RELEASED: 15th June 1992
RETIRED: 15th July 1992
EDITION SIZE: 18,854
SIZE: Width: 5" Depth: 4 ¹/₂" Height: 7"
MARKINGS: © DAVID WINTER 1992
ISSUE PRICE: £150 $275

PLUM COTTAGE

I nitially this lovely thatched piece was intended solely for direct mail order selling by John Hine Limited in the UK, through advertisements in *Country Living* magazine (October & November 1993 issues). The response was not too successful and so Plum Cottage was offered as a "seasonal special" to retailers in a limited edition of 4,500, at the higher price of £49.95 and $90. The piece was retired on 24th December 1993. The name is a tribute to one of England's most celebrated writers, P.G. Wodehouse (the creator of Jeeves), whose nickname was 'Plum'.

SCULPTED: 1993
RELEASED: October 1993
RETIRED: December 1993
EDITION SIZE: 4,500
SIZE: Width: 4 ¹/₂" Depth: 3 ¹/₂" Height: 4 ⁷/₈"
MARKINGS: © DAVID WINTER 1993
ISSUE PRICE: £40 $50

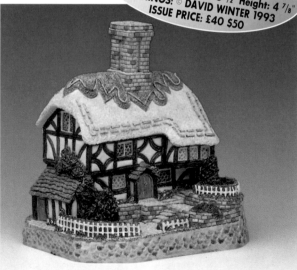

WINTERSHILL
(Jim 'll Fix It)

SCULPTED: 1987
RELEASED: 1987/8 RETIRED: 1988
EDITION SIZE: 250
SIZE: Width: 4" Depth: 3 ¾" Height: 4 ⅛"
MARKINGS: © DAVID WINTER 1987
ISSUE PRICE: £200 $375

In 1987, 10-year old Jody Jackman wrote to the BBC's 'Jim'll Fix It' programme asking if her mother Penny could see how David Winter Cottages are made. The programme (broadcast on 27th February 1988) showed Penny watching David sculpt a model of the Jackman's own home in Framlingham, Hampshire, explaining the various production processes involved, and finally watching Audrey White paint the finished model. Afterwards an edition of 250 was released at £200 ($375) each, the proceeds of the sales going entirely towards the rebuilding of London's Great Ormond Street Children's Hospital. John Hine presented Sir Jimmy Saville with a cheque for £50,000 on TV during a subsequent edition of 'Jim 'll Fix It'. The name 'Wintershill' was created for the piece and is now also the name of the Jackman's real house.

CHRISTMAS COLLECTION

EBENEZER SCROOGE'S COUNTING HOUSE

SCULPTED: 1987
RELEASED: 1987
RETIRED: February 1988
SIZE: Width: 5" Depth: 4 ⅝" Height: 6"
MARKINGS: © DAVID WINTER 1987
ISSUE PRICE: £43 $97

David has sculpted a special Christmas piece every year since 1987, and this was the first. The piece was very popular and availability stretched from September '87 through till 29th February '88. All subsequent Christmas pieces have been retired on 31st December when all production moulds are destroyed. Watch out for a distinctive variation to the piece. Early models have a small bush at the rear, at the point where the central and clock tower buildings adjoin. On later pieces the bush was extended much further upwards, almost approaching the snow-covered gable. This modification was made to prevent the two sections from separating in the mould (Fairytale Castle is another example of the technique).

SCULPTED: 1988
RELEASED: 1988
RETIRED: 31st December 1988
SIZE: Width: 6" Depth: 4 3/8" Height: 5 1/2"
MARKINGS: © DAVID WINTER 1988
ISSUE PRICE: £46 $100

CHRISTMAS IN SCOTLAND AND HOGMANAY

To date, the only special Christmas piece not inspired by Charles Dickens' *A Christmas Carol* . Available from September to 31st December (Hogmanay) 1988. John Hine personally destroyed the production moulds by feeding them to the Loch Ness Monster (yes, really!). Note the icicles hanging from the roof; made from strands of clear resin.

A CHRISTMAS CAROL

SCULPTED: 1989
RELEASED: 1989
RETIRED: 31st December 1989
SIZE: Width: 6 3/8" Depth: 4 5/8" Height: 5 3/4"
MARKINGS: © DAVID WINTER 1989
ISSUE PRICE: £46 $135

A favourite of many collectors, A Christmas Carol was the special Christmas piece for 1989. It was also the first to have a specially printed box.

MR FEZZIWIG'S EMPORIUM

SCULPTED: 1990
RELEASED: 1990
RETIRED: 31st December 1990
SIZE: Width: 5" Depth: 4 1/2" Height: 6"
MARKINGS: © DAVID WINTER 1990
ISSUE PRICE: £60 $135

David can be seen sculpting this piece, the 1990 Christmas 'special', on the video produced by John Hine Studios called *MEET THE ARTIST*. Mr Fezziwig was young Scrooge's employer, a jovial character whose premises are described as a warehouse in the story *A Christmas Carol*, but 'emporium' sounds much nicer. His trade is never specified by Dickens. (According to the Muppets version he sold rubber chickens.)

FRED'S HOME . . .

Full title: *Fred's Home - "Merry Christmas, Uncle Ebenezer," said Scrooge's nephew Fred, "and a Happy New Year."* — decided upon after *Tiny Tim's House* and *Bob Cratchit's Dwelling* were considered and rejected. The long title was devised to explain immediately to one and all who Fred is. Keen-eyed collectors will notice that Scrooge's first name is spelt with an extra 'e' (Ebeneezer) on the customised box for this piece. Even keener-eyed owners of the video *MEET THE ARTIST* may observe the piece (blocked-up but without detail) lurking in the background on some of the scenes in David Winter' studio. The video was filmed in the summer of 1990, so David was clearly well ahead of schedule with the special piece for Christmas 1991.

SCULPTED: 1991
RELEASED: 1991
RETIRED: 31st December 1991
SIZE: Width: 5" Depth: 4 ⁵/₈" Height: 7 ⁵/₈"
MARKINGS: © DAVID WINTER 1990
ISSUE PRICE: £60 $145

SCROOGE'S SCHOOL . . .

SCULPTED: 1992
RELEASED: 1992
RETIRED: 31st December 1992
SIZE: Width: 5" Depth: 4 ¼" Height: 6 ½"
MARKINGS: © DAVID WINTER 1992
ISSUE PRICE: £75 $160

The special piece for Christmas 1992. Full title: *Scrooge's School — wherein young Ebenezer learnt more about loneliness and grief than Latin and Greek.* Another long name, to indicate it was during his painful school years that Scrooge's miserly nature was formed. The metal bell in the bell tower has a tendency to drop off.

OLD JOE'S BEETLING SHOP

SCULPTED: 1993
RELEASED: 1993
RETIRED: 31st December 1993
SIZE: Width: 4 ¾" Depth: 4 ½" Height: 7 ¾"
MARKINGS: © DAVID WINTER 1993
ISSUE PRICE: £75 $175

The special piece for Christmas 1993. Old Joe is the pawnbroker whom Scrooge oversees bartering for his own belongings in the would-be future. 'Beetling' means either that the building was overhanging the street outside or that the stamping of clothes with wooden hammers went on within it's rickety walls.

127

CHRISTMAS ORNAMENTS

The three sets of Christmas Ornaments released annually between 1991 and 1993 are reduced reworkings of David Winter Cottages sculpted for John Hine Studios by Hilary Macdonald and produced in the Far East. According to John Hine Studios, the reason for making them outside the UK is that higher domestic production costs would have made the project impossible. Hanging versions (with a hook and string attached) were also available but not in the USA. Three of the 1992 set (Fairytale Castle, Suffolk House, Tudor Manor House) were given a sprinkling of snow which did not appear on David's originals.

1991 SET

Scrooge's Counting House
SCULPTED: 1991
RELEASED: September 1991
RETIRED: December 1991
SIZE: W: 1 7/8" D: 1 1/2" H: 2"
MARKINGS: JHL © 91
(plus plaque: 1987)
ISSUE PRICE: £6 $15

Hogmanay
SCULPTED: 1991
RELEASED: September 1991
RETIRED: December 1991
SIZE: W: 2 1/4" D: 1 5/8" H: 1 7/8"
MARKINGS: JHL © 91
(plus plaque: 1988)
ISSUE PRICE: £6 $15

A Christmas Carol
Sculpted: 1991
RELEASED: September 1991
RETIRED: December 1991
SIZE: W 2" D: 1 3/8" H: 1 3/4"
MARKINGS: JHL © 91
(plus plaque: 1989)
ISSUE PRICE: £6 $15

Winner of Best Ornament of the Year Award by NALED (National Association of Limited Edition Dealers), USA, 12th July 1992.

Mr Fezziwig's Emporium
Date Sculpted: 1991
Date Released: September 1991
Date Retired: December 1991
SIZE: W: 1 5/8" D: 1 1/2" H: 1 7/8"
MARKINGS: JHL © 91
(plus plaque: 1990)
ISSUE PRICE: £6 $15

1992 SET

Fred's Home . . .
SCULPTED: 1992
RELEASED: September 1992
RETIRED: December 1992
SIZE: W: 1 1/2" D: 1 1/2" H: 2 3/8"
MARKINGS: © DW 92
(plus plaque: 1991)
ISSUE PRICE: £7.50 $15

Fairytale Castle
SCULPTED: 1992
RELEASED: September 1992
RETIRED: December 1992
SIZE: W: 1 1/2" D: 1 1/4" H: 2 1/2"
MARKINGS: © DW 92
ISSUE PRICE: £7.50 $15

Suffolk House
SCULPTED: 1992
RELEASED: September 1992
RETIRED: December 1992
SIZE: W: 1 5/8" D: 1 1/4" H: 1 7/8"
MARKINGS: © DW 92
ISSUE PRICE: £7.50 $15

Tudor Manor House
SCULPTED: 1992
RELEASED: September 1992
RETIRED: December 1992
SIZE: W: 1 3/4" D: 1 1/4" H: 1 5/8"
MARKINGS: © DW 92
ISSUE PRICE: £7.50 $15

1993 SET

Scrooge's School
SCULPTED: 1993
RELEASED: September 1993
RETIRED: December 1993
SIZE: W: 1 5/8" D: 1 1/4" H 2"
MARKINGS: © DW 93
ISSUE PRICE: £7.50 $15

Tomfool's Cottage
SCULPTED: 1993
RELEASED: September 1993
RETIRED: December 1993
SIZE: W: 1 3/4" D: 1 5/8" H: 1 3/4"
MARKINGS: © DW 93
ISSUE PRICE: £7.50 $15

The Grange
SCULPTED: 1993
RELEASED: September 1993
RETIRED: December 1993
SIZE: W: 1 3/4" D: 1 3/8" H: 1 3/4"
MARKINGS: © DW 93
ISSUE PRICE: £7.50 $15

Will-'o-the-wisp
SCULPTED: 1993
RELEASED: September 1993
RETIRED: December 1993
SIZE: W: 2" D: 1 1/4" H: 2"
MARKINGS: © DW 93
ISSUE PRICE: £7.50 $15

The 1993 set of Christmas Ornaments.

Section
Three

Rareties, One-offs, The Unusual

The items listed in this section are also the work of David Winter. The first ten are extremely rare, either because they were produced in very small edition sizes or because they were 'one-offs' cast for special occasions; a slight exception is the Village Scene Point-of-Sale, which was made in larger numbers and has established a track record on the secondary market. The remaining items never entered production and were not released commercially by John Hine Studios.

(An additional shop display stand featuring the logos of David Winter Cottages and John Hine Limited and the wording FINEST MINIATURE HOUSES also exists and is known to have sold on the secondary market. However, the piece is not included here as it is the work of Steve Kenyon and Paul Easton - not David Winter.)

> DATE SCULPTED: 1991
> DATE RELEASED: 1991
> SIZE: Width: 6 $^5/_8$" Depth: 5 $^5/_8$" Height: 11"
> MARKINGS: © DAVID WINTER 1991
> CURRENT VALUE: Unknown

BRONZE CASTLE IN THE AIR

In the same year that CASTLE IN THE AIR was released, a special one-off was produced in cold cast bronze — a mixture of powdered bronze (70%) and resin (30%) — to commemorate The London Collectors Showcase, a two day show held in October 1991. The piece was offered in silent auction and sold for £2,600 to a syndicate of three prominent UK collectors. In every respect it is identical to the conventional model, with the exception of a tiny modification known only to John Hine Studios, added to ensure authenticity. In 1994 the owners were looking for a buyer who would be prepared to pay in the region of £9,000.

Photograph courtesy of John Hine Ltd.

BRONZE CHICHESTER CROSS

A Chichester Cross was cast in bronze by David Winter for display at an exhibition in The Maltings, Farnham, Surrey in 1981. From the display model, orders were taken and the edition closed at just six pieces. The exhibition had been organised to reflect the work of numerous artists who all live in David's village.

DATE SCULPTED: 1981
DATE RETIRED: 1981
SIZE: Width: 3 ½" Depth: 3 ½" Height: 4 ¼"
MARKINGS: None
ISSUE PRICE: £45 $N/A
CURRENT VALUE: £4500+
$6000-7500

BRONZE ST PAUL'S CATHEDRAL

SCULPTED: 1981
LOCATION: 19 Ash Street
RELEASED: 1981 RETIRED: 1982
SIZE: Width: 5 ⅝" Depth: 3 ¼" Height: 3 ½"
MARKINGS: None
ISSUE PRICE: £20 $N/A
CURRENT VALUE: Unknown

A bronze version of the model sculpted to commemorate the 1981 Royal Wedding was produced and is believed to be limited to just eight pieces. The number reflects lack of sales rather than a deliberate low edition, and this piece appears on company order forms of the time as part of the collection.

BRONZE OLD JOE'S BEETLING SHOP

DATE SCULPTED: 1993
SIZE: Width: 4 ¾" Depth: 4 ½" Height: 7 ¾"
MARKINGS: © DAVID WINTER 1993
CURRENT VALUE: Unknown

A special one-off in cold cast bronze, produced this time as a prize for a charity raffle held during CARNIVAL '93 in Warwick, October 1993. The lucky winner was a collector from Buckinghamshire, England.

EICH DYN

Before it was renamed Y Ddraig Goch (The Red Dragon), this piece from the Welsh Collection was going to be called 'The Prince of Wales' and on the pub sign were the words EICH DYN, the Prince's motto, and three feathers, his emblem. But Welsh speakers at the Wrexham workshops pointed out that the motto is in fact ICH DIEN, which is German for 'I SERVE'. EICH DYN makes sense in Welsh — it means 'My Man' — and the confusion arises from the fact that EICH DYN is apparently an ancient spelling of ICH DIEN. Anyway, to save further linguistic mix-up, the name was changed totally, to Y Ddraig Goch, before any production pieces were made. At least two EICH DYNs exist, both in resin. One is the original painting master (which is the property of John Hine Studios); the other was made as a prize for the same charity raffle as the bronze Old Joe's at CARNIVAL '93 and won by a collector from Bedfordshire, England.

SCULPTED: 1993
LOCATION: Home Studio
RELEASED: 1993
SIZE: Width: 6 ¼" Depth: 3 ⅛" Height: 4"
MARKINGS: © DAVID WINTER 1993
CURRENT VALUE: Unknown

GREEN LANES

Green Lanes is the name of the only private commission ever undertaken by David. His friend, Nicholas Rink, asked for a model of his own house as a Christmas present, and so David set to work at short notice, sculpting, mouldmaking and casting in a great hurry. Using a single rubber block mould he cast the one-and-only model. John Hine took it home with him, dried the piece over night by placing it on a storage heater and then painted it himself on Faith Winter's dining room table. Delivery to Mr Rink was made in person on Christmas Eve. The piece has come to be known as in David Winter circles as Green Lanes, but the name of the actual building is Greenlane House.

SCULPTED: 1980
SIZE: Width: 8" Depth: 3" Height: 3"
CURRENT VALUE: Unknown

CARD DISPENSER

SCULPTED: 1984
LOCATION: Home Studio
RETIRED 1984
SIZE: Width: 10" Depth: 4 ½" Height: 8 ½"
ISSUE PRICE: Unknown
CURRENT VALUE: Unknown

A point-of-sale on which to display the Collectors' Catalogue Cards (See section on Memorabilia). Very few were made and they are now extremely rare. They were not terribly robust and many broke at the point where they were glued together (David sculpted it in two halves).

Photograph courtesy of John Hine Ltd.

CANDLEHOLDER BASE FOR COACHING INN

A nother rare curiosity — a hollow base for The Coaching Inn with holes around the edge for six candles. It was sculpted in plasticine by David Winter, rather than his usual wax, and from the original the few that were cast were sold in the run-up to Christmas 1980.

SCULPTED: 1980
LOCATION: The Coalshed
RETIRED 1980
SIZE: Width: 15 ½" Depth: 11" Height: 2 ½"
ISSUE PRICE: Unknown SN/A
CURRENT VALUE: Unknown

Photo: Patty and Bill Sauers

VILLAGE SCENE
(Point-of-Sale)

T he original point-of-sale from which the first complementary Guild piece derived. The only difference is the wording on the plaque, which in this case reads 'David Winter Cottages.' (The Guild piece reads 'David Winter Cottages Collectors Guild.') This piece was never released to the public; however collectors have been known to persuade stores to part with them and they do appear for sale on the secondary market.

SCULPTED: 1986
LOCATION: 19 Ash Street
SIZE: Width: 10" Depth: 4 ½" Height: 8 ½"
MARKINGS: None
ISSUE PRICE: £0 $0
CURRENT VALUE: £130-175
$250-450

STRATFORD HOUSE IN TERRACOTTA

SCULPTED: 1981
LOCATION: Home Studio
RETIRED 1981
SIZE: Width: 6 ¼" Depth: 4" Height: 4 ⅝"
ISSUE PRICE: Unknown $N/A
CURRENT VALUE: Unknown

The same exhibition at the Farnham Maltings for which David cast the bronze Chichester Cross also saw a version of Stratford House in terracotta. He used these unpainted examples of his work to emphasize the purely sculptural forms. Again a display model was cast from which orders were taken. The exact number cast remains in doubt. Two are definitely known to exist; one is in a private collection in the USA, the other (the display model marked 'Number One' by David on the base) belongs to Faith Winter.

UNRELEASED PIECES

With the exception of the variety of bits and pieces listed below — there are to date only two Cottages in existence which David sculpted but have never been released — The Lighthouse and O'Reilly's Bar. Both were intended for the original Irish Collection and were set aside when he postponed work on it in 1990.

THE LIGHTHOUSE

David was never happy with this piece whilst sculpting it and did not think it representative of his work. When the Irish Collection was postponed the piece was suggested as a possible Guild piece and the base marking changed. In the event David sculpted Will-'o-the-wisp as Guild Piece No. 10. The Lighthouse bears a strong resemblance to the Fastnet Lighthouse off the coast of Southern Ireland.

SCULPTED: 1990
SIZE: Width: 4" Depth: 3 ¾" Height: 7 ½"
MARKINGS: Guild No. 10
© DAVID WINTER 1990

Photograph courtesy of John Hine Ltd.

Photograph courtesy of John Hine Ltd.

O'REILLY'S BAR

I t's a shame this lovely thatched Irish pub never saw the light of day. The example in this book is one of a number of painting test samples which were made, although final colours were never approved. The piece never went into production.

OTHER ITEMS

19 ASH STREET

D avid's model of the proposed extension to the garage at 19 Ash Street which John Hine presented to the local Planning Department in lieu of conventional architect's drawings. Planning permission was refused, due partly, it would seem, to this unconventional approach. The piece sat in John Hine's office for a long while and was even used as a door stop. It is still in John's possession but is nowadays treated with a little more reverence.

CUSTOMISED COAL SHED

G uild Piece No. 6, The Coal Shed, with the front and side walls cut away to reveal the detail within. Just one model was adapted in this way for photographic purposes.

Rareties, One-offs, The Unusual

POINT OF SALE

The very first point-of-sale consists of a section of roofing and the top of a chimney with the words 'David Winter Cottages' lying across the tiles. The piece dates from the early 1980s and was never sold commercially. Examples are very rare indeed.

VILLAGE SCENE WITH BACK

SCULPTED: 1986/7
RELEASED: 1991
MARKINGS: © DAVID WINTER 1986

The spire on the top of Village Scene has a tendency to snap off and this experimental piece was created in an attempt to alleviate the problem when the piece was launched as the first complementary Guild piece in 1987. The idea was not pursued and did not reach painting stage.

Photograph courtesy of John Hine Ltd.

WINDING ROAD

A thread of road sculpted for photographic purposes to link pieces in the Irish Collection. The picture was intended for use in the Guild magazine, Cottage Country, with David superimposed walking along the road. Nice idea but it never happened.

Photograph courtesy of John Hine Ltd.

LOST FOREVER

AN IRISH COTTAGE: David blocked up a cottage whilst preparing the original Irish Collection but was not satisfied with the results and melted the wax down for re-use. No photographs or design notes exist.

PHONEBOX: In 1980 David sculpted a British telephone box and his wax original sat around in the coalshed for a long while gathering dust. No casts were ever made of it and the piece is now lost.

WILLIAM SHAKESPEARE'S DEATHPLACE: A simple tombstone marked R.I.P., sculpted in 1982 by David in mischievous mood when everyone seemed to be having a go at modelling William Shakespeare's Birthplace (Tim Moore, Malcolm Cooper, David himself).

Comparisons

A picture speaks a thousand words, and there is no better way of comparing different versions of pieces than by viewing them side by side. The following series of photographs demonstrate a variety of points to help collectors identify mould variations and other alterations.

SINGLE OAST

Mould 1 (left) and Mould 2 — the original 1981 and restyled 1985 versions. Mould 1 is smaller in size and has neither foliage nor white fencing; some examples also have a grey roof. (The same differences apply to Moulds 1 & 2 of Triple Oast.)

TUDOR MANOR HOUSE

Front and rear views of the 1981 Mould 2 (left) and 1985 Mould 4. Note the disappearing name plaque, the height of the chimneys, plus the marginally smaller size and general 'aged' appearance of Mould 2. Far right: Two side views of the very rare 1981 Mould 1, showing the walkway passing right through the building, which was blocked up on subsequent versions.

Courtesy of Martin Winter

▲ Mould 1 (right) and Mould 2 — original
1980 and restyled 1983 versions. At a
glance the pieces seem fairly similar,
but closer inspection reveals that most
of the detail has been reworked; the
tiles on the roof are a good example —
crisper and more prominent.

▼ Mould 2 (left) and Mould 3 — dating
from 1980 and 1983. These are the two
most commonly found versions, the significant difference being the change from
beamwork to weatherboarding on the
shop front. (The very rare Mould 1 has
the same weatherboarding as Mould 3.)
On the later version greenery can be
seen growing up the right side, and the
chimney is taller.

THE WINEMERCHANT

Comparisons

CHICHESTER CROSS

The two original colour variations — stone grey (left) and stone white. Sandstone buff and the bronze came later.

W. SHAKESPEARE'S BIRTHPLACE

Three versions of the same piece: the large and 'tiny' pieces are by David Winter, the medium-sized is by Malcolm Cooper.

THE WINDMILL

A rare early version (right) with only six frames per sail (sails cast in injection moulded plastic), and the standard later version with seven frames per sail (sails cast in metal).

Comparisons

BROOKSIDE HAMLET

THE BAKEHOUSE

Early version courtesy of Stuart and Sally H.

SUFFOLK HOUSE

▲ An early 1982 version (right) and one of the last pieces to be made by John Hine Studios in 1991. Note the water dripping from the waterwheel on the later version.

◄ A standard production piece (left) and a very early version made in 1983 with the different chimney style and extra row of bricks at the top of the stack.

◄ Colour variations make a difference to the price of this piece — 'whites' are more valuable than 'pinks' (which can be found in pale and dark shades).

Comparisons

QUAYSIDE

An early (left) and late version: the pieces did not change during production but the difference in painting style clearly demonstrates the contrast between early soft tones and the later, bolder colours which had developed by the mid-eighties.

ROSE COTTAGE

A side view of the 1980 Mould 1 (left) and 1985 Mould 2 — original and restyled versions. On the later version the flowers creeping up the wall and the tiny window between the two levels of thatch are missing.

▼ Mould 1 (left) dating from 1983 and a Mould 2 cast in 1992. The main difference to be aware of is the narrower courtyard of the rare early version.

HERTFORD COURT

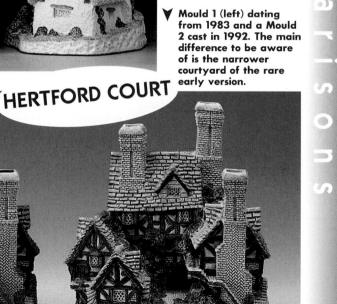

Early version courtesy of Carol and Howard Barnett

E.SCROOGE'S COUNTING HOUSE

Rear view showing the extended bush growing up the back wall on later versions (right) to prevent the two main sections of the piece from separating in the mould.

Mould 2 (left) and Mould 3 — the main difference is the loss of the name plaque (The Castle Keep) on the later version, and there are variations to the windows. On the original version, Mould 1, the name plaque read 'Guildford Castle'.

CASTLE KEEP

Mould 2 version courtesy of Brian Gourlay.

▼ Moulds 1,2,3 and 4 have a variety of glass effects covering the intricate window display. This picture shows Mould 3 (left), using clear acetate for glass, and Mould 5 which has no glass effect and the display beyond blocked in.

OLD CURIOSITY SHOP

TYTHE BARN

Below: Two examples of Mould 1 ('door on') showing how the position of the right hand barn door varies; interesting colour variations, too. Left is a picture of Mould 2 ('door off').

Wrap-around sleeve courtesy of David Winter

ST PAUL'S CATHEDRAL

Two colour variations of the piece sculpted to commemorate the 1981 Royal Wedding, plus the wrap-around sleeve for the box (complete with spelling mistake — 'minature').

▼ **Two versions demonstrating the copious amounts of foliage added to later versions, notably on the church and on cottage roofs.**

Cotswold Village

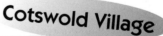

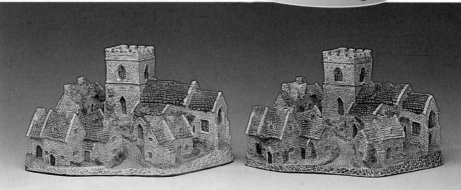

comparisons

15 LAWNSIDE ROAD

On the left, the piece as it was released, with rendering to the left side; on the right, an experimental pre-production version with beams all round which was never released.

IVY COTTAGE

Early version courtesy of Heather Lavender

THE VILLAGE SHOP

▲ Two versions produced by John Hine Studios — one in the mid-eighties (left) with ivy spreading onto the roof, and another in 1993 with the ivy removed. Numerous other variations also exist.

◀ Two examples of the same piece, with no variations or modifications, but cast and painted a decade apart — one in 1983 (right), the other in 1993.

M e m o r a b i l i a

This section lists books, promotional material, plates, toby jugs, plates and ephemera associated with David Winter Cottages.

BOOKS & OTHER PRINTED MATERIAL

COLLECTORS' CATALOGUE CARDS
(1984)

A pack of 40 cards each having a picture of a Cottage on one side and text on the other. One card contains text about David Winter plus a photograph of him at work sculpting Castle Gate. Look carefully and you will notice that the piece varies considerably from the finished piece; he had yet to crumble away part of the castle walls and add the cottages in the foreground.
ISSUE PRICE: £1.50 $5
CURRENT PRICE: £100-150 $400-500

THE COLLECTORS BOOK
(1985)

A small, square pocket book extremely popular with collectors. Contains colour illustrations of pieces currently available plus text along the lines of the Certificates of Authenticity. Interesting short story based on Brookside Hamlet. Revised,

updated and renamed COLLECTORS' CATALOGUE before going out of print in 1989. Hardback only.
ISSUE PRICE: £5 $10

COLLECTING DAVID WINTER COTTAGES (1989)
by John Hine

John Hine's personal account of the first ten years of David Winter Cottages written in his own highly entertaining style. Contains photographs and text on all pieces available at the time plus photographs of the retired pieces (but no text). Published by John Hine Studios. Hardback only. A special limited edition bound in leather was also produced.
ISSUE PRICE: £15 $40

COLLECTORS POCKET BOOK
(1989)

A soft-covered booklet with a reddish-brown wood effect on the cover (also used on 1989 promotional leaflet which contains same pictures of the 'regional' collections). Includes photographs of all current pieces plus text and information on how the Cottages are made, up to and

including the British Traditions collection and the 1989 Christmas piece, A Christmas Carol.
ISSUE PRICE: £5 $8

RETIRED RANGE BINDER
(1989)

A harback ring binder containing photographs of retired pieces, but no text. An update pack was produced in 1990, but no more have been forthcoming since.
ISSUE PRICE: £20 $40

THE TALE OF PERSHORE MILL
(1991)
by John Hine

A beautifully illustrated fable written by John Hine and inspired by David's 1991 complementary Guild piece. The characters in the illustrations are portrayed mostly by people who worked for John Hine Studios at the time; one of them, Sir Walter de Comberton, is David Winter. A signed limited edition was made available to Guild members.
ISSUE PRICE: £14.95 $29.95

THE DAVID WINTER COTTAGES HANDBOOK
1992/93 (1992)
by John Hughes

The first official price guide to David Winter Cottages. Contains pictures and text on all pieces up to and including Cameos and the Irish Collection, plus a price guide to the secondary market as it stood in Spring 1992. Published by Kevin Francis Publishing.
ISSUE PRICE: £14.95 $29.95

THE DIRECTORY
(1992)

A card index box featuring all pieces produced by September 1992, current and retired, with a clever sticker system for instant updating when new pieces are discontinued. An update pack was being planned but not yet available in spring 1994.
ISSUE PRICE: £29.95 $65

PROMOTIONAL MATERIAL
(1980-1994)
All produced by John Hine Studios.

1980
FRONT COVER: *DAVID WINTER COTTAGES* plus profile portait of David at work by his sister Alice. Inside are line drawings of all 1980 pieces except The Coaching Inn (mentioned but not illustrated).
Format: 4"x3" cream booklet, four stapled pages.

1981
FRONT COVER: *DAVID WINTER COTTAGES* plus same portrait as 1980 by Alice Winter. Contains illustrations of what are described in the text as "thirty-four miniature cottages evoking the spirit of rural life from days gone by." Features The Village as "David Winter's special piece for Christmas 1981." Format: single A3-size cream sheet folded to A5 (8 3/4" x 5 1/4").

1982/3
Simple sheet listing all currently available pieces.
Format: single A4-size sheet folded to A5.

1984
FRONT COVER: *FLIGHTS OF FANCY. DAVID WINTER COTTAGES — THE COLLECTION.* includes colour (for the first time) illustrations of 35 pieces, but not all 1984 pieces (Snow Cottage and Tollkeeper's Cottage are missing).

1985
FRONT COVER: *DAVID WINTER COTTAGES - THE COLLECTION.* First leaflet to feature a date — 1985. Illustrations of 55 pieces including the 10-strong Heart of England series.
Format: single A3-size brown sheet folded to A5.

1986
FRONT COVER: *DAVID WINTER COTTAGES - THE COLLECTION* plus map of the UK; colour - pale blue. Includes boxed photographs of pieces with each double-page including text and sepia illustration of a craftsman at work (blacksmith, spinner, basketmaker, carpenter, cooper). Falstaff's Manor is shown but no other '86 pieces (West Country Collection weren't released until '87).
Format: A5-size, 12 pages, stapled, landscape

1988
FRONT COVER: *DAVID WINTER COTTAGES -*

AN INTRODUCTION FROM JOHN HINE STUDIOS plus photograph of Falstaff's Manor. Format and contents uncertain.

1988
FRONT COVER: *DAVID WINTER COTTAGES - FINE ENGLISH COLLECTIBLES* plus photograph of Lacemaker's; colour - purple. Includes photographs of 67 pieces including The Grange and the new Scottish Collection. Features new Studios and Workshops of John Hine Limited logo for the first time. Produced by John Hine Studios in USA for North American distribution.
Format: 8 1/2" X 3 1/2" folding out to 20 1/2" x 11"

1989
FRONT COVER: *DAVID WINTER COTTAGES - FINEST MINIATURE HOUSES - THE COLLECTION* plus Studios and Workshops of John Hine Limited logo; colour - same reddish-brown wood effect as the Collectors Pocket Book. Features the West Country, Midlands, Scottish, British Traditions collections with a inside back-page foldout for the Main Collection. Back page features special 1989 Christmas piece, A Christmas Carol. Also published in several European languages (the German version includes such delightful names as 'Derbyshire Baumwollspinnerei' and 'Falstaff's Landgut'.)
Format: 8" x 5", 12 pages, stapled.

1991
FRONT COVER: *DAVID WINTER COTTAGES* ; colour - pale blue. Released early in 1991 for a UK trade show and then modified before general release.
Format: 8" x 3 1/2", stapled, landscape.
FRONT COVER: *DAVID WINTER COTTAGES - ARTIST OF THE YEAR* Features all pieces in the current range as at winter 1991. The title refers to the 'Artist of the Year' award bestowed on David Winter by the National Association of Limited Edition Dealers in the USA.
Format: 8" x 4", 10 pages concertina-style.

1992
(All 1992 front covers feature the *DAVID WINTER COTTAGES* logo)
FRONT COVER: *NEW RELEASES* plus illustration of harvest scene. Dated on back cover - 8th January 1992.
Format: A4-size, single fold-out.

FRONT COVER: *NEW FOR JAN '92*
Format: 8" x 4", 8 pages, stapled.
Format: 8" x 4", 20 pages, stapled.
FRONT COVER: *DAVID WINTER CAMEOS*
Features the 12 miniatures and diorama in two paint styles.
Format: 8" x 4", 6 pages, stapled.
FRONT COVER: *DAVID WINTER COTTAGE - NEW RELEASES AUTUMN AND WINTER 1992* plus illustration of cottage fireside scene.
Format: A4-size, single fold-out.

1993

(All 1993 front covers feature the *DAVID WINTER COTTAGES* logo)
FRONT COVER: *THE SHIRES - NEW FOR 1993* ; colour - pale yellow with feint line illustration.
Format: 8" x 4", double fold-out.
FRONT COVER: *NEW RELEASES - SPRING 1993* plus illustration of spring countryside scene with green border.
Format: A4-size, single fold-out.
FRONT COVER: *NEW RELEASES - AUTUMN & WINTER 1993* plus illustration of autumn scene with swans and purple border.
Format: A4-size, single fold-out.

1994

FRONT COVER: *DAVID WINTER COTTAGES - CURRENT RANGE 1994* plus photographs of four pieces (Inglenook Cottage, The Bakehouse, The Weaver's Lodgings, Moonlight Haven). Contains all pieces current up to and including The English Village.
Format: 11" x 8", 12-pages, stapled.

OTHER ITEMS

TABLE MATS & COASTERS
(1984)

Both available in a set of six with matching colour illustrations (by Micheal Fisher) of David Winter Cottages on each — The Dower House, The Bakehouse, Stratford House, The Bothy, Tudor Manor House and Sussex Cottage. produced for John Hine Studios by the Clover Leaf company, launched in August 1984 and available for approximately two years. Prototypes of a set of four larger mats for North America were made but never released. Plans to reissue the original sets in 1991 were cancelled

due to the adverse effect this would have on secondary market prices; a new set with new illustrations was considered but discarded.
ISSUE PRICE: £10 $30 (Set of six table mats)
CURRENT PRICE: £150-300 $300-400
ISSUE PRICE: £8 $13 (Set of six coasters)
CURRENT PRICE: £75-150 $150-250

THE GUILD PIPE & SMOKING KIT
(1987)

Pipe smoker's paraphernalia produced in very small quantities, a byproduct of an article in an early issue of the Guild magazine (Winter '87) about pipe makers. The pipe, tobacco, leather pouch and wooden pipe rack were all embossed with the word 'Guild'.
ISSUE PRICES: Pipe - £32 $50; Tobacco per tin - £3.50 $ 6; Pouch - £27 $43; Pipe Rack - £90 $ 145.

DAVID WINTER ROCK
(1988)

A stick of great British seaside rock specially made to accompany an article in the Guild magazine (Summer '88) and offered free to collectors who contributed to the Letters Page. Each of the 200 sticks made had David Winter's name written through the centre.

VIDEO - 'MEET THE ARTIST'
(1990)

Highly recommended — an excellent insight into how David Winter works on his Cottages with long sequences

n which he just talks and sculpts in his studio. John Hine has some very interesting points to make, so too does the late Audrey White. The female narrative is a little overdone in places, but a minor fault in an otherwise excellent production. Playing time: approx. 30 minutes.
ISSUE PRICE: £10 $20

DAVID WINTER TOBY JUG
(1991)

Sculpted by Doug Tootle and produced by Kevin Francis Ceramics as one of their series of Great Artists and Potters. David's figure is seen sitting on Blossom Cottage and holding The Dower House; the handle is a pipe standing on its end, on top of which sits a sleepy mouse reading a book. A limited edition of 950 were made.
ISSUE PRICE: £250 $450
CURRENT PRICE: £250-400 $500-700

PERSHORE MILLER TOBY JUG
(1992)

Sculpted by Ray Noble and inspired by John Hine's book *The Tale of Pershore Mill*. John himself portrayed the Pershore Miller in the book illustrations and the toby jug depicts him sitting on a bag of flour holding David's sculpture of Pershore Mill. John's dogs are at his side (they also appear in the book) and the handle is a flour sack with the miller's wicked son Jasper peering out (as portrayed by sculptor Janet King). A limited edition of 1,500 were made, each supplied with a complementary copy of *The Tale of Pershore Mill*.
ISSUE PRICE: £150 $ 300

GUILD SWEAT SHIRTS
(1992)

Dark blue sweat shirts made exclusively for John Hine Studios and sold direct from the Guild offices. On the front is the David Winter Cottages Guild logo and on the back the words *John Hine Studios*. Three sizes: Medium, Large & Extra Large. Probably no longer available.
ISSUE PRICE: £19.95 $29.95

THE DAVID WINTER PLATE COLLECTION

A series of plates created in limited editions for John Hine Studios by Villetta China of Houston, Texas. Each plate features an illustration, by British artist Micheal Fisher, of a retired David Winter Cottages in an imaginary setting. Each plate is individually hand numbered.

A Christmas Carol
RELEASED: 1991
EDITION: 10,000
(Closed)
ISSUE PRICE: £18 $30

Cotswold Village
RELEASED: 1991
EDITION: 10,000
(Closed)
ISSUE PRICE: £18 $30

Chichester Cross
RELEASED: 1992
EDITION: 10,000
ISSUE PRICE: £18 $30

Little Mill
RELEASED: 1992
EDITION: 10,000
ISSUE PRICE: £18 $30

The Old Curiosity Shop
RELEASED: 1992
EDITION: 10,000
ISSUE PRICE: £18 $30

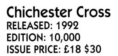

E. Scrooge's Counting House	Dove Cottage	The Forge	House On Top	Tythe Barn
RELEASED: 1992	RELEASED: 1993	RELEASED: 1993	RELEASED: 1993	RELEASED: 1993
EDITION: 10,000	EDITION: 10,000	EDITION: 10,000	EDITION: 10,000	EDITION: 10,000
ISSUE PRICE: £18 $30	ISSUE PRICE: £18 $30	ISSUE PRICE: £18 $30	ISSUE PRICE: £18 $30 Production Cancelled	ISSUE PRICE: £18 $30 Production Cancelled

MISCELLANEOUS

VILLAGE MEMORIES
(1989)

A one-off issue of a magazine comprising excerpts from the first eight issues of Cottage Country, intended for general bookshop/newsagent distribution.

BURNS POETRY
(1989)

An audio cassette of Robert Burns poems. Produced in 1989 at the time of the British Traditions collection, to complement Burns' Reading Room.

THE MAIDS OF PERSHORE MILL
(1991)

A song composed by John Hine to promote the launch of his book *The Tale of Pershore Mill* . A small quantity of audio cassettes were released.

MAD BARON FOURTHRITE'S SPECTACULAR
(1992)

Video
John Hine's stage show at South Bend, Indiana, July 1992, recreated on video. Inspired by David's sculpture Mad Baron Fourthrite's Folly. Running time: 1 hour (approx.) but seems longer.
ISSUE PRICE: £9.95 $19.95

Audio Cassette
The songs and music from the stage show linked with brief narration by John Hine. Running time: 20 minutes (approx.)
ISSUE PRICE: £4.95 $9.95

MAD BARON FOURTHRITE'S FAMILY HISTORY & BARONESS HARDUNBUY'S BOOK OF HAPPY TIMES AHEAD
(1992)

Two booklets written by John Hine to complement Mad Baron Fourthrite's Folly. Available only as a pair.
ISSUE PRICE: £3.50 $6.50

BADGES (BUTTONS), PINS, TILES AND WATCHES

In the UK they're called 'badges', in America 'buttons'; either way, a variety of them exist, some produced by John Hine Studios and others by stockists or collectors clubs. The most commonly available is a David Winter Cottages Collectors Guild badge (slightly different versions in UK and North America) which is still currently available.

Pins and tiles featuring pictures of David Winter Cottages have been produced by a number of stockists, and since 1991 John Hine Studios have sold a gold plated Mouse Pin (Issue price: £2.95 / $5.00). A David Winter wrist watch (featuring the DWC logo on the face) has also been produced by stockist Marvin Korngut of Collectors Haven in Los Angeles, California.

Memorabilia

Animal Corner

One of the great pleasures of collecting David Winter Cottages is to discover the secret of the mouse . . . a delightful hidden detail that David sculpts onto his work.

The story goes that in 1982 David was sculpting away, adding the finishing touches to Brookside Hamlet at the Hendon Road workshop in Bordon. Another artist who was working for John Hine Limited at the time, David Tate, had just completed a model of a mouse sitting on a piece of cheese. David Winter thought it looked more like a rat and sculpted a small mouse on the side of Brookside Hamlet to make his point. It stayed there, and by chance the mouse was born.

He then proceeded to add the mouse to many (but not all) of his sculptures, a secret trade mark as it has been for others before. Artist Terence Cuneo signs his paintings with a tiny mouse and Yorkshire furniture maker Robert Thompson sculpted a mouse onto one of his pieces in the 1930s and began a tradition which is still continued by his company today.

The mouse has never been talked about officially. Collectors have been left to discover the secret for themselves. To this day there has never been official recognition from John Hine Studios that it even exists! Their stock reply to questioning is: "Mouse? What Mouse?"

Then in 1991 the mouse disappeared (last seen on CASTLE IN THE AIR) and an owl took its place. The owl supposedly ate the mouse and there is a piece on which the mouse's tail can be seen dangling from the owl's beak! The owl lurks in bushes and is even trickier to find than its predecessor.

When collectors discovered what had happened, they were appalled at the loss of their old friend and petitioned John Hine Studios. By popular demand the mouse returned two years later; he can be seen again for the first time on the 1993 Guild plaque, On The Riverbank. On the same piece you can see the owl flying away.

If this is all news to you and you have an overwhelming urge to go hunting with a magnifying glass, Brookside Hamlet is recommended as the piece to start with — the first mouse is also the biggest and easiest to spot.

This list of where to find mice and owls is not intended to spoil anyone's fun (you don't have to read it if you don't want to!) but it might save long, frustrating hours if you just can't manage to spot the little blighters. More importantly, it's best to know if there isn't one at all!

On The Church and Vestry (English Village collection) the mouse seems to have found himself a partner. Could there be offspring to follow . . . ?

MOUSE AND OWL HUNT CHECKLIST

With acknowledgement to Pat Hinckle and Simon Connolly for their help in compiling the list.

THE ALMS HOUSES - Mouse above doorway on larges house.
ANNE HATHAWAY'S COTTAGE - None
THE APOTHECARY SHOP - None
ARCHES THRICE - Mouse on rear wall, between buildings.
ASHE COTTAGE - Mouse in walkway to front porch.
AUDREY'S TEA ROOM/SHOP - Owl in top of bush on chimney, at rear.
THE BAKEHOUSE - Mouse on back of chimney.
BARLEY MALT KILN - Owl on bush, left side, next to corner shed.
THE BEEKEEPER'S - Owl under eaves by chimney.
BERKSHIRE MILKING BYRE - Mouse on step next to churns.
BIRTH DAY COTTAGE - Mouse on left bank at rear.
BIRTHSTONE WISHING WELL - Owl in top of bush on chimney.
(A) BIT OF NONSENSE - See Llanfairpwllgwyngyllgogerychwrndrobwllllantysilio-gogogoch

BLACK BESS INN - Mouse on top of step at rear.
BLACKFRIARS GRANGE - None
BLACKSMITH'S COTTAGE - None
BLOSSOM COTTAGE - Mouse in front of flower pot, right front.
THE BOAT HOUSE - Mouse on ground, right side.
THE BOTHY - Mouse at base of chimney at rear.
THE BOOKBINDERS - See Bookends
BOOKENDS - Mouse on windowsill of Bookbinders.
BOTTLE KILN - Mouse in doorway of kiln on right.
BROOKLET BRIDGE - Owl half way up tree at rear.
BROOKSIDE HAMLET - Mouse on rocks at back, above David Winter's name.
BUCKINGHAMSHIRE BULL PEN - Mouse on wall, right of gate
THE BULL AND BUSH - Mouse on lower windowsill, left side.

151

BURNS' READING ROOM - Mouse on left side of chimney, near the pots.

THE CANDLEMAKER'S - Owl in bush under eaves at rear, by the chimney.

CARTWRIGHT'S COTTAGE - None

THE CASTLE COTTAGE OF WARWICK - None (or incredibly well hidden).

CASTLE IN THE AIR - Mouse on battlements, right side. Owl in foliage above.

CASTLE KEEP - None

CASTLE GATE - On back of tallest turret.

THE 'CAT AND PIPE' INN - Mouse on top of chimney at front.

THE CHANDLERY - Mouse on windowsill at rear.

THE CHAPEL - None (mouse chased away by ghosts in the graveyard)

CHESHIRE KENNELS - Mouse on wall at right, beside kennels.

CHICHESTER CROSS - None

(A) CHRISTMAS CAROL - Mouse on upper windowsill, left front.

CHRISTMAS IN SCOTLAND AND HOGMANAY - Mouse on windowsill below clock.

CHRISTMAS ORNAMENTS - None

THE CHURCH AND VESTRY - Two mice on heart-shaped cobble stone at rear.

THE COACHING INN - None

THE COAL SHED - Mouse peeping out of OXO box, inside.

THE COBBLER - Mouse at base of chimney.

THE CONSTABULARY - Mouse on left side windowsill at rear.

THE COOPER'S COTTAGE - Mouse at rear on right side, on first board.

CORNISH COTTAGE - None

CORNISH ENGINE HOUSE - Mouse on windowsill of shed.

CORNISH HARBOUR - Mouse on right side, on third white step.

CORNISH TIN MINE - Mouse at rear on rocks in middle.

COTSWOLD COTTAGE - None

COTSWOLD FARMHOUSE - None

COTSWOLD VILLAGE - Mouse on far right front windowsill of church.

THE COTTON MILL - Mouse on stairs to right.

CRAFTSMEN'S COTTAGES - None

CROFTERS COTTAGE - Mouse on rock ledge, right side, halfway up.

CROWN INN - None

CRYSTAL COTTAGE - Mouse on back step.

DERBYSHIRE COTTON MILL - Mouse in black part of chimney stack.

DERBYSHIRE DOVECOTE - Mouse in far left dovecote opening.

DEVON COMBE - Mouse on seat in boat.

DEVON CREAMERY - Mouse on wall at bottom of steps, right side.

DOUBLE OAST - None

DOVE COTTAGE - None

DOWER HOUSE - None

DROVER'S COTTAGE - None

EBENEZER SCROOGE'S COUNTING HOUSE - Mouse on windowsill of middle front window.

THE ENGINE HOUSE - Mouse at rear on brick wall near chimney.

FAIRYTALE CASTLE - Mouse next to ivy at base of tallest tower.

FALSTAFF'S MANOR - Mouse on right front windowsill.

FISHERMAN'S WHARF - Mouse on left chimney.

FOGARTYS - Owl in middle of bush at rear, near back door.

FRED'S HOME . . . - Mouse on front middle windowsill, above door.

THE FORGE - None

GATEKEEPERS - Mouse on back window of round tower.

GILLIE'S COTTAGE - Mouse in front of dog kennel.

GLEBE COTTAGE - Mouse outside right front door.

GLOUCESTERSHIRE GREENHOUSE - Mouse on bench inside greenhouse.

THE GRANGE - Mouse in doorway on second floor, beyond metal balcony.

GREENWOOD WAGON - Owl in top of tree, at rear above © symbol.

THE GREEN DRAGON INN - Mouse on rock at base, above date marking at rear.

GROUSE MOOR LODGE - Mouse on lower roof, front right.

GUNSMITHS - Mouse in archway on third step.

GUY FAWKES - Mouse in front of double doors, right side.

THE HALL - Mouse on left side of brick wall.

HAMPSHIRE HUTCHES - Mouse on lower set of steps, at doorway.

HARVEST BARN - Mouse on windowsill, right side.

THE HAYBARN - None

HERMITS HUMBLE HOME - Mouse on top of pot by base of tree at rear.

HERTFORD COURT - Mouse on landing, front right.

THE HOGS HEAD TAVERN/BEER HOUSE - None

HOME GUARD - Mouse on front left window of bunker.

HORATIO PERNICKETY'S AMOROUS INTENT - Owl, top middle of the ivy at rear, beneath railing.

HOUSE OF THE MASTER MASON

THE HOUSE ON THE LOCH - Mouse on seat in boat.

HOUSE ON TOP - Mouse in cave entrance, left front.

INGLENOOK COTTAGE - Owl in bush above rocks on side where cross beams cross.

IRISH ROUND TOWER - Owl in top of tall bush growing up side of tower.

IRISH WATER MILL - Owl on back, mid-left bush.

IVY COTTAGE - None

JOHN BENBOW'S FARM HOUSE - Mouse by barn door, back of wood pile.

KENT COTTAGE - Mouse by door frame on left side.

KNIGHT'S CASTLE - Mouse on top windowsill, right side.

LACEMAKERS - Mouse peeking out under blowing curtain.

LANCASHIRE DONKEY SHED - Mouse on bale of hay.

(15) LAWNSIDE ROAD - Mouse on brick wall at right side.

LITTLE FORGE - None

LITTLE MARKET - None

LITTLE MILL (all versions) - None

LLANFAIRPWLLGWYNGYLLGOGERYCHWYRNDROBWLLLLAN-
TYSILIOGOGOGOCH - see A Bit of Nonsense

LOCK-KEEPER'S COTTAGE - Mouse in the barge.

LYCH GATE - Owl in bush above Copyright marking.

MACBETH'S CASTLE - Mouse on top of turret.

MAD BARON FOURTHRITE'S FOLLY - None (must have departed with Baroness Hardunbuy)

MARKET DAY - Owl on right side of bush at rear.

MARKET STREET - Mouse on right chimney top.

MEADOWLANE COTTAGES - None

THE MILL HOUSE (original / remodelled) - None

MINER'S COTTAGE - None

(COAL)MINERS ROW - Mouse in right cave.

MISTER FEZZIWIG'S EMPORIUM - Mouse on bush, right side.

MOONLIGHT HAVEN - Mouse on edge of right chimney.

MOORLAND COTTAGE - None

MURPHYS - Owl in top of bush on chimney.
O'DONOVAN'S CASTLE - Owl in mid bush near window, at rear.
THE OLD CURIOSITY SHOP - None
THE OLD DISTILLERY - Mouse at base of tallest chimney, at rear.
OLD JOE'S BEETLING SHOP - Mouse on stone at rear left corner.
ON THE RIVERBANK - Mouse on ledge of left lower window.
ONE ACRE COTTAGE - Mouse at rear on last step, left side.
ONE MAN JAIL - Owl in tree.
ONLY A SPAN APART - Owl in top of bush over Copyright marking.
ORCHARD COTTAGE - Mouse on fence, right side.
OXFORDSHIRE GOAT YARD - Mouse on shed roof.
THE PARSONAGE - Mouse on cupola windowsill, right side.
PATRICK'S WATER MILL - See Irish Water Mill
THE PAVILION - Mouse on steps, rear right corner.
PEN-Y-GRAIG - Mouse in cave with baskets at rear.
PENNY WISHING WELL - Owl in bush, top left side.
PERSHORE MILL - Mouse on swinging arm above double doors.
PILGRIM'S REST - Mouse on top windowsill at rear.
THE PLUCKED DUCKS - Mouse on windowsill, far right.
PLUM COTTAGE - Mouse on the ground at rear, to left of back door
THE POST OFFICE - Mouse on right side stone wall.
THE POTTERY - Mouse at rear of top chimney ledge.
THE POTTING SHED - Owl in mid bush at wall.
POULTRY ARK - Owl in bush on left side, near the ark.
THE PRINTERS - See Bookends
THE PRIVY - Owl on bush behind door.
PROVENCAL A - None
PROVENCAL B - None
PROVENCAL ONE - None
PROVENCAL TWO - None
PUDDING COTTAGE - Mouse on top left front windowsill.
THE QUACK'S COTTAGE - Mouse on large cobblestone step at rear.
QUAYSIDE - None
QUEEN ELIZABETH SLEPT HERE - Mouse on second step, right side.
THE RECTORY - None
ROBIN HOOD'S HIDEAWAY - Mouse in knothole in main tree trunk.
ROSE COTTAGE - None
SABRINA'S COTTAGE - None
SADDLE STEPS - Mouse in top of tree, at rear.
ST ANNE'S WELL - Mouse on top of lower wall.
ST GEORGE'S CHURCH - None
ST NICHOLAS' CHURCH - None
ST PAUL'S CATHEDRAL - None
SCENES
AT THE BAKEHOUSE - Mouse on left side front, second step.
AT THE BOTHY - Mouse on left side, on top of grey wall.
AT ROSE COTTAGE - Mouse on top of last stepping stone.
CHRISTMAS SCENE - Mouse on third step up, first flight of stairs.

THE SCHOOLHOUSE - None
SCOTTISH CROFTERS - Mouse on rock ledge, right side, halfway up.
SCROOGE'S SCHOOL . . . - Owl at rear, in ivy over middle

patch of snow, left of CHRISTMAS '92.
SECRET SHEBEEN - Owl on left side, in top of bush to the right.
THE SEMINARY - Mouse on left of roof at rear.
SHIREHALL - None
SHROPSHIRE PIG SHELTER - Mouse on third log, right end.
SINGLE OAST - None
THE SMITHY - Mouse on elevated ledge outside door, right side
SMUGGLERS CREEK - Mouse on end of flat horizontal rock near pinnacle.
SNOW COTTAGE - Mouse on brick ridge around top of chimney.
SPINNER'S COTTAGE - None
SQUIRES HALL - Mouse on top of chimney, near pots, at rear.
STAFFORDSHIRE STABLE - Mouse on wall beyond cat.
STAFFORDSHIRE VICARAGE - Mouse on ornamental bric work, at rear.
STONECUTTER'S COTTAGE - Mouse on left of chimney, near pot.
STRATFORD HOUSE - None
STREET SCENE (Bas Relief Plaque) - Mouse on windowsill, right side of street.
SUFFOLK HOUSE - Mouse on roof by chimney.
SULGRAVE MANOR - None
SUSSEX COTTAGE - None
SWAN UPPING COTTAGE - Mouse on lower part of chimney at rear.
TAMAR COTTAGE - Mouse in small cave, on ground.
THAMESIDE - Mouse between plants over bay window, right side.
THE TANNERY - Mouse on rear left windowsill
THERE WAS A CROOKED HOUSE - Mouse confronting cat outside front door.
THREE DUCKS INN - None
TOLLKEEPER'S COTTAGE - Mouse on the wooden bridge.
TOMFOOL'S COTTAGE - Mouse on brickwork below basement window.
TRIPLE OAST - Mouse on left oast in roof corner.
TUDOR MANOR HOUSE - None
TYDDYN SIRIOL - Mouse on right side, top step of landing to right of open door.
TYTHE BARN - None
THE VICARAGE - None
THE VILLAGE - None
VILLAGE SCENE - Mouse next to steeple window.
THE VILLAGE SHOP - None
THE WEAVER'S LODGINGS - None
WELSH PIG PEN - Owl in top of bush at rear.
WHILEAWAY COTTAGE - Mouse in archway on chimney at side.
WILLIAM SHAKESPEARE'S BIRTHPLACE (Large) - None
WILLIAM SHAKESPEARE'S BIRTHPLACE (Tiny) - None
WILL-'O-THE-WISP - Mouse on back right windowsill.
WILTSHIRE WATERWHEEL - Mouse on wall in front of waterwheel.
THE WINDMILL - None
THE WINEMERCHANT - None
WINTERSHILL (Jim'll Fix It) - Mouse on top of chimney, beside stacks.
WOODCUTTERS COTTAGE - Mouse on far right branch holding up top cottage.
Y DDRAIG GOCH - Mouse in front on path, right side.
YEOMAN'S FARMHOUSE - None
YORKSHIRE SHEEP FOLD - Mouse on wall to left of gate.

Eggars Hill and other Places to Visit

EGGARS HILL

Eggars Hill is *the* place to visit for ardent collectors. The home of David Winter Cottages was established in 1987 and is housed in restored buildings set around a delightful courtyard garden. The original intention was that Eggars Hill should function as the creative heart of John Hine Studios in contrast to the workshop activities at Bordon and Wrexham. To a certain extent this is still true, but its prime importance today is as a vistors centre.

The most impressive part of Eggars Hill is the seventeenth century wooden barn, completely restored and protected in a shell of glass and brick. Here visitors can see a display of almost every piece David Winter has ever sculpted (including very rare retired pieces), plus the work of other John Hine Studios artists. They can also witness demonstrations of how the Cottages are made and make purchases at the in-house shop.

Tours of Eggars Hill are free of charge and include morning coffee or afternoon tea. They commence at 10 am and 2 pm seven days a week. During the busy summer months and holiday times, it is advisable to reserve a tour in advance to avoid disappointment.

You are welcome to visit:
JOHN HINE STUDIOS
Eggars Hill
2 Hillside Road
Aldershot
Hampshire GU11 3NB
TEL: (0252) 334672

GLADSTONE POTTERY MUSEUM

This is the museum visited by David Winter prior to sculpting Bottle Kilns and there is a strong resemblance between his piece and the museum buildings. The exhibits give a detailed account of the history of the

Eggars Hill

Staffordshire pottery industry, with craftsmen demonstrating their skills.

Gladstone Pottery Museum
Uttoxeter Road
Longton
Stoke-on-Trent
Staffordshire

WELSH FOLK MUSEUM

On the outskirts of Cardiff, Wales, you can see the real buildings which inspired several of David's sculptures; The Haybarn, Welsh Pig Pen, Miners Cottage. They are all exhibits at an excellent open air museum which contains buildings rescued from all over Wales and re-erected in the grounds of St Fagan's Castle. Even without the David Winter connection it's well worth a visit.
Welsh Folk Museum, St Fagan's, Cardiff, South Wales

WHITBREAD HOP FARM

A mecca for anyone fascinated by oast houses and probably the largest grouping of oasts in the world. David sculpted a single, double and triple - but this one has twelve! It's a museum nowadays and the added incentive for a visit is that they stock David Winter Cottages!
Whitbread Hop Farm, Beltring, Paddock Wood, Tonbridge, Kent TN12 6PY

Collectors Clubs and useful Publications

CLUBS

Independent Collectors Clubs sprang up like mushrooms in the late 1980s and have done a magnificent job in generating enthusiasm for collecting David Winter Cottages by holding meetings and other social events, exchanging news and (in some cases but not all) publishing regular newsletters. Club members tend to be the first to acquire information about new products and are generally the most informed collectors around.

The following are some of the clubs worldwide that operate independently of John Hine Studios and are known to be currently active:

USA

DAVID WINTER COTTAGES COLLECTORS CLUB
FLORIDA
Gulf Coast Chapter - 1111 83rd Street N.W.,
Bradenton, Florida 34209 *Contact: Jo Ann Murdoch.*
DAVID WINTER COTTAGES CLIQUE OF MIDDLE GEORGIA
1931 Rocky Creek Road, Macon, Georgia 31210 *Contact: Tanzel Rousey.*
DAVID WINTER COLLECTORS CLUB OF WASH-INGTON-BALTIMORE
14815 Peppertree Drive, Bowie, Maryland 20721 *Contact: Arthur Pipek.*
DAVID WINTER CLUB
Metro Michigan - 29939 Old Bedford, Farmington Hills, Michigan 48331
Contact: Helene Friedman.
DAVID WINTER COTTAGES COLLECTORS CLUB
Central Michigan Area - 1614 Applecroft Lane, Mason, Michigan 48854
Contact: Ellen Wigginton.
DAVID WINTER COTTAGES CLUB
Toledo Area Chapter - P.O. Box 112, Perrysburg, Ohio 43551
Contact: Sue Rawson.
DAVID WINTER COLLECTORS CLUB OF NORTH-ERN VIRGINIA
P.O.Box 301, Fairfax, Virginia 22030
Contact: Jim Coates.
DAVID WINTER CLUB OF CENTRAL VIRGINIA
6501 Centralia Road, Chesterfield, Virginia 23832 *Contact: Beverly Karnes.*
EMILY'S COTTAGE CLUB
14855 Clayton Road, Chesterfield, Missouri 63017 *Contact: Michele Fenno.*

EUROPEAN TREASURES COLLECTORS SOCIETY
4205 Murray Avenue, Pittsburg, Pennsylvania 15217 *Contact: Sue Harmon.*
JOHN HINE COLLECTIBLES CLUB
Foothills Chapter - 2461 West 299th Place, Torrance, California 90501
Contact: Judy Lacey.
JOHN HINE COLLECTIBLES CLUB
Orange County Chapter - P.O. Box 8531, Fountain Valley, California 92708
Contact: Ken Tomb
JOHN HINE COLLECTIBLES CLUB
Inland Empire Chapter - 8919 Randolph, Riverside, California 92503
Contact: Rose McFarlin.
JOHN HINE COLLECTIBLES CLUB
San Diego Chapter - 5487 Camanito Bord, San Diego, California 92108 *Contact: Joe Walther.*
JOHN HINE COLLECTIBLES CLUB
Farmers Market Chapter - Collectors Haven 6333 W. 3rd Street, Los Angeles, California 90036 *Contact: Esther Kamm.*
JOHN HINE COLLECTIBLES CLUB
Metro Chapter - P.O. Box 2004, Rivervale, New Jersey 07675 *Contact: Ted Camhi.*
SUPERIOR CALIFORNIA COLLECTORS CLUB
P.O. Box 231785, Sacramento, California 95823 *Contact: Sherry Greener.*
PACIFIC NORTHWEST DAVID WINTER CLUB
12018 S.E. 51st, Bellevue, Washington 98006 *Contact: Jim Howton.*

UNITED KINGDOM

DAVID WINTER COLLECTORS CLUB - UK
66 Bridgewood Road, Worcester Park, Surrey KT4 8XR *Contact: Ann Hamlet.*

COLLECTABLES COLLECTORS CLUB
3 East Street, Littlehampton, West Sussex
BN17 6AU
Contact: Heather Lavender.

AUSTRALIA

Details of Australian clubs (John Hine
Collectors Club - Victoria Chapter *[contact —
Neil Dennis]*, Winter In Wollongong *[contacts
— Sandra and Guido Bainat]*, The
Harboursiders *[contact — Maureen Clarke]*
and possibly others) can be obtained from
the Australian Guild Coordinator:
Bev Munro — Royal Selangor (Aust) Pty Ltd.,
15 Gatwick Road, P.O.Box 566, Bayswater,
Victoria 3153. Tel: (613) 720 7199
Fax: (613) 720 7127

PERIODICALS

COTTAGE COUNTRY

Back issues of the Guild magazine, *Cottage
Country* , are full of information useful to
collectors and it's worth trying to get hold
of a complete set for reference. Certain
issues are now quite rare, notably the first
four (1987), and 21 and 22 (Spring/Summer
'92). John Hine Studios sell back issues of
any stocks they have via their Guild Offices.

Other independent magazines which
contain Cottage information may be worth
subscribing to:

COLLECTORS MART

650 Westdale Drive, Wichita, Kansas 67209
USA
Phone: (316) 946 0600
Fax: (316) 946 0675
Bimonthly, dedicated to collectibles. Has
ads for DW dealers and classified section,
including many secondary market listings.

COLLECTOR EDITIONS

170 Fifth Avenue, New York, New York
10010 USA
Phone: (212) 989 8700
Bi-monthly, dedicated to collectibles.
Regular ads for DW dealers.

THE ANTIQUE TRADER

PO Box 1050, Dubuque, Iowa 52001 USA
Phone: (319) 588 2073
Weekly newspaper aimed primarily at the
antiques market but includes several pages
of classified ads for collectibles. Also extensive list of upcoming shows and auctions.

COLLECTORS NEWS

17 Clare Avenue, Woodbridge, Suffolk
IP12 4ES ENGLAND
Bi-monthly, includes ads for DW dealers.

EXCHANGE AND MART

Link House, 25 West Street, Poole, Dorset
BH15 1LL ENGLAND
Phone: (0202) 671171
Sometimes used by collectors and dealers in
the UK to buy and sell Cottages.

CANDIAN COLLECTIBLES

(Formerly 'Insight on Collectibles')
103 Lakeshore Road Suite 262, St
Catharines, Ontario L2N 2T6 CANADA

NEWSPAPERS

THE DAILY TELEGRAPH (UK), STARS & STRIPES
(Europe), THE AUSTRALIAN (Australia), USA
TODAY (USA), THE GLOBE & MAIL (Canada).
John Hine Studios have placed announce-
ments in these newspapers on the last
Thursday of every month since January
1992, often declaring the instant retirement
of David Winter Cottages. Dealers and collectors have climbed on board and regularly
advertise in the same column on that day,
providing a good source of contacts for
buying and selling. John Hine Studios
monthly advertisement will probably cease
during 1994.

Clubs and Publications

Index of Cottages

Index of Cottages